T0328202

Cambridge Elements ≡

Elements in the Philosophy of Mind
edited by
Keith Frankish
The University of Sheffield

EMBODIED AND ENACTIVE APPROACHES TO COGNITION

Shaun Gallagher
*University of Memphis and
University of Wollongong*

CAMBRIDGE
UNIVERSITY PRESS

Shaftesbury Road, Cambridge CB2 8EA, United Kingdom

One Liberty Plaza, 20th Floor, New York, NY 10006, USA

477 Williamstown Road, Port Melbourne, VIC 3207, Australia

314–321, 3rd Floor, Plot 3, Splendor Forum, Jasola District Centre,
New Delhi – 110025, India

103 Penang Road, #05–06/07, Visioncrest Commercial, Singapore 238467

Cambridge University Press is part of Cambridge University Press & Assessment,
a department of the University of Cambridge.

We share the University's mission to contribute to society through the pursuit of
education, learning and research at the highest international levels of excellence.

www.cambridge.org
Information on this title: www.cambridge.org/9781009209809

DOI: 10.1017/9781009209793

© Shaun Gallagher 2023

This work is in copyright. It is subject to statutory exceptions and to the provisions
of relevant licensing agreements; with the exception of the Creative Commons version
the link for which is provided below, no reproduction of any part of this work may take
place without the written permission of Cambridge University Press & Assessment.

An online version of this work is published at doi.org/10.1017/9781009209793 under
a Creative Commons Open Access license CC-BY-NC 4.0 which permits re-use,
distribution and reproduction in any medium for non-commercial purposes providing
appropriate credit to the original work is given and any changes made are indicated.
To view a copy of this license visit https://creativecommons.org/licenses/by-nc/4.0

All versions of this work may contain content reproduced under license from third
parties. Permission to reproduce this third-party content must be obtained from these
third-parties directly.

When citing this work, please include a reference to the DOI 10.1017/9781009209793

First published 2023

A catalogue record for this publication is available from the British Library.

ISBN 978-1-009-20980-9 Paperback
ISSN 2633-9080 (online)
ISSN 2633-9072 (print)

Cambridge University Press & Assessment has no responsibility for the persistence
or accuracy of URLs for external or third-party internet websites referred to in this
publication and does not guarantee that any content on such websites is, or will
remain, accurate or appropriate.

Embodied and Enactive Approaches to Cognition

Elements in the Philosophy of Mind

DOI: 10.1017/9781009209793
First published online: July 2023

Shaun Gallagher
University of Memphis and University of Wollongong
Author for correspondence: Shaun Gallagher, s.gallagher@memphis.edu

Abstract: This Element discusses contemporary theories of embodied cognition, including what has been termed the "4Es" (embodied, embedded, extended, and enactive cognition). It examines diverse approaches to questions about the nature of the mind, the mind's relation to the brain, perceptual experience, mental representation, sensemaking, the role of the environment, and social cognition, and it considers the strengths and weaknesses of the theories in question. It contrasts embodied and enactive views with classic cognitivism, and discusses major criticisms and their possible resolutions. This Element also provides a strong focus on enactive theory and the prospects for integrating enactive approaches with other embodied and extended theories, mediated through recent developments in predictive processing and the free-energy principle. It concludes with a brief discussion of the practical applications of embodied cognition. This title is also available as Open Access on Cambridge Core.

Keywords: cognition, embodied, embedded, extended, enactive

© Shaun Gallagher 2023

ISBNs: 9781009209809 (PB), 9781009209793 (OC)
ISSNs: 2633-9080 (online), 2633-9072 (print)

Contents

1 Introduction: What Is Embodied Cognition (EC)?

Generally speaking, theorists of embodied cognition (EC) claim that the body's neural and extraneural processes, as well as its mode of coupling with the environment, play important roles in cognition. Embodied cognition has philosophical roots in phenomenology and pragmatism, but also incorporates insights from analytic philosophy of mind, and is richly informed by research in developmental and experimental psychology, the neurosciences, and robotics. Perhaps because of this diversity of disciplines and viewpoints, the concept of EC is not a settled one. Although EC is usually portrayed as a challenge to classic Cartesian and cognitivist accounts that have dominated and continue to dominate theoretical approaches to the mind, this is not always the case. Embodied cognition includes a variety of approaches ranging from conservative versions that stay close to standard computational models of the mind, to more radical, nonrepresentationalist accounts that oppose narrow neurocentric theories.

To help us map out the theoretical territory encompassed by EC, and its relation to classic cognitivism (CC), that is, cognitive science approaches that emphasize internal computational or mental representational processes, I propose to use a modified set of questions specially designed for this purpose by Alvin Goldman and Frederique de Vignemont (2009: 158). They present a clear challenge to EC theorists to clarify what is meant by embodiment and embodied cognitive processes. I will refer to them as *challenge questions*, and paraphrase them as follows: Under the selected interpretation of EC:

1. Which notion of embodiment is operative?
2. Which sectors of cognition, or which cognitive tasks, are embodied; and how fully does each task involve embodiment?
3. What empirical evidence supports specific embodiment claims?
4. How do the proffered claims depart substantially from CC?
    I will add a fifth question, closely related to (4).
5. What role do mental or neural representations play in cognition?

Answers to these questions can guide our understanding of both the theoretical and practical stakes involved in different conceptions of EC.

First, however, we need to identify a list of candidate theories that fall under the broad heading of EC. It is both a help and a hindrance that so many reviews of EC start by offering a catalog of different approaches. It's helpful in the sense that they make some good distinctions among candidate approaches, but it's a hindrance in the sense that the lack of consensus about terminology and principles of classification generates some important ambiguities. Still, examining such attempts to characterize the field of EC will facilitate our introductory task by clarifying the scope of the various issues that will concern us in the following sections. As I review these attempts, and as I map out the field of EC, I'll return several times to the challenge questions.

2 The Field of EC

Let us start with Margaret Wilson's (2002) early characterization of "six views of embodied cognition." These "views" could rightly be thought of as a set of principles that different approaches to EC might selectively embrace. I'll label them W for Wilson, 1–6.

(W1) cognition is situated (the environment in which it happens plays a significant role)

(W2) cognition is time-pressured

(W3) we offload cognitive work onto the environment

(W4) the environment is part of the cognitive system

(W5) cognition is for action

(W6) offline cognition is body-based.

Different theories of EC will emphasize different subsets of these claims, while rejecting others. Larry Shapiro (2007: 338), accordingly, prefers to call EC "a *research programme*, rather than a *theory*, ... to indicate that the commitments and subject matters of EC remain fairly nebulous." He lists three research goals for EC, which identify three different emphases:

(S1) An emphasis on the contribution of physical bodily processes to the *process* of cognition

(S2) An emphasis on the contribution of bodily factors to the *content* of cognition

(S3) An emphasis on the importance of body–environment coupling for cognition.

If we divide Wilson's six by Shapiro's three, the issues start to multiply: W6 is clearly related to S2. Both Wilson and Shapiro have in mind the work of Lakoff and Johnson (1999), who show how offline, higher-order cognition is grounded in bodily metaphors, or in body-related brain simulations, as found in the work of Lawrence Barsalou (1999), Arthur Glenberg (2010), and others (see Section 3.1 for a discussion of these approaches). If there is good agreement on this point, agreement is less clear on the other claims. Under S3, Shapiro mentions only the concept of extended mind (Clark & Chalmers 1998). Should it also include Wilson's claims about situated (W2) and action-oriented (W5) cognition? It's not clear. It's also not clear that S1 is covered by any of Wilson's claims, or that W2 fits with any of Shapiro's goals. There are other lists that expand the inventory of issues to include, for example, robotic bodies and artificial agents (e.g., Ziemke 2001).

For our purposes, the point is not to refine these lists, but to notice the wide variety of themes, issues, and approaches covered by EC. Indeed, rounding out approximately twenty years of attempts to classify forms of EC, Shapiro and Spaulding (2021), referencing Wilson, warn that trying to reduce the numbers "risks generalizing the description of embodied cognition to the extent that its purported novelty is jeopardized."

Perhaps the most influential attempt to define the field of EC has been the idea of 4E cognition (Menary 2010c; Newen, De Bruin, & Gallagher 2018; Rowlands 2010). The 4E (embodied, embedded, extended, and enactive) concept involves a minor ambiguity, however. On the one hand, it is an attempt to characterize generally different approaches to EC; on the other hand, it includes "embodied" cognition as one specific kind of approach. In addition, it has become customary to note that there are more than four Es that should be included in any comprehensive account of the mind; for example, ecological, emotional, empathic, existential, and so on.

Although no one classificatory scheme can do full justice to the complexity involved in EC, for the purposes of the following discussions I adopt the 4E schema. It is important to note several limitations or qualifications attached to this strategy. First, there are many convergence points as well as disagreements among the 4Es. For example, we can find principles from ecological psychology being taken up in all four of the 4E approaches. And although affect or emotion-related processes are clearly emphasized in the first E (embodied), they also play a prominent part in enactive accounts. Likewise, body–environment coupling may be central to embedded, extended, and enactive approaches, even if defined somewhat differently by each one. Such differences can be important. For example, an embedded approach would claim that environmental factors can have only a causal influence on cognition; extended and enactive approaches often claim that in some circumstances environmental factors contribute constitutively to cognition. This is the difference between Wilson's W3, where we offload cognitive work onto the environment, allowing the environment to play a causal role, and W4, where the environment is considered to be part of the cognitive system.[1] In addition, from one E to the next, there is

---

[1] Shapiro and Spaulding (2021: n.p.) point out that the concept of body–environment coupling has several meanings, but that ecological and enactive approaches share a technical definition of coupling expressed in terms of dynamic systems theory.

no strong consensus on what weight to give to basic concepts such as embodiment or representation.

Moreover, contrary to what is typically assumed, not all EC approaches share a common opposition to the classic cognitivism model of cognition. This is a contentious issue. If the standard computational model of cognition trades on the idea that mental processes are computational processes that operate across representations, and is committed to the internalist, neurocentric conception that cognition is always "in the head," EC in most (but not all) versions rejects one or both of these commitments and emphasizes the significance of bodily processes, and of interactions with the environment, for cognitive systems.

In addition, different 4E approaches propose different ways in which the body plays a role in shaping cognition. On one view, the nonneural body processes information prior to and subsequent to central or neural manipulations (e.g., Chiel & Beer 1997); on another view, minimal, action-oriented representations do some of the work (Clark 1997; Wheeler 2005); and on still another conception, the body itself plays a representational role (Rowlands 2006). In contrast, enactive approaches suggest that posture and bodily movement, including sensorimotor contingencies (i.e., how sensory processes respond to bodily movement; O'Regan & Noë, 2001), and bodily affectivity (Colombetti 2014) all enter into cognition in a nonrepresentational way. For some, the idea that the body is dynamically coupled to the environment is important (Di Paolo 2005; Thompson 2007); for others, the idea that action affordances are body- and skill-relative is essential (Chemero 2009). These ideas, to one degree or other, help to shift the ground away from orthodox cognitive science. In general terms, it's not just the brain but the brain–body–environment that is agentive in cognition. Even if this is the broad message of EC, in some versions of EC the material and structural aspects of embodiment are discounted, and cognition continues to be characterized in terms of internal representations, as we'll see in the next section.

If these are differences that distinguish the different E-approaches, it is also important to note that there are also significant differences to be found within each of the Es. Within the first E, for example, there has been a distinction made between "weak" embodiment, which stays close to computational and

---

The behaviors of objects are coupled when the differential equations that describe the behavior of one contains a term that refers to the behavior of the other. ... The co-occurrence of terms in the equations that describe a dynamical system shows that the behavior of the objects to which they refer are co-dependent. They are thus usefully construed as constituents of a single system – a system held together by the interactions of parts whose relationships are captured in coupled differential equations.

As such, the coupling relation is considered to be constitutive of cognition. I discuss this claim in Section 7.1.

representational models, and "strong" embodiment, which rejects those standard models. Within embedded approaches one can distinguish between emphases on environmental constraints (where external factors impinge on the agent) versus ecological relationality (where factors count only in their tight relation with the agent). Within discussions of extended mind, one can define two, three, or even four versions or "waves," some of which endorse conceptions of computation and representation; and within enactive approaches, there are distinctions between autopoietic and radical enactivism, although they both share an antirepresentationalist approach.

Hence the need for a good map. In the following sections I will explore in more detail the EC landscape, focusing on the 4Es, and I'll try to show how each one answers the challenge questions we started with. Starting in Section 6, I'll focus more closely on enactive approaches to cognition.

3 The First E: Embodiment

Adrian Alsmith and Frederique de Vignemont (2012) distinguish between "weak" and "strong" embodiment. Strong embodiment endorses a significant explanatory role for the (nonneural) body in cognition; weak embodiment gives a significant explanatory role to body-related or body-formatted (neural) representations. Indeed, for weak EC, the body per se – including its anatomical, postural, kinetic, and more general physical features – is not necessarily involved in cognitive processes. Rather, all the real and relevant action occurs in the brain. Except for the brain, this version of EC is strikingly disembodied; embodiment signifies, at best, the "body in the brain" (Berlucchi & Aglioti 2010; Tsakiris 2010).

3.1 Weak EC

Alvin Goldman, building on research in psychology, neuroscience, linguistics, and philosophy, has given the most developed account of what he calls a "unifying and comprehensive" account of EC (2012: 85). On his view, however, actual bodies play a marginal and perhaps even trivial role in cognition. Rather, body-formatted (or B-formatted) representations in the brain do most of the work. Goldman thus rules out aspects of anatomy, sensorimotor contingencies, and environmental couplings as relevant to cognition, and he makes it clear that "[t]he brain is the seat of most, if not all, mental events" (Goldman & de Vignemont 2009: 154). The processes involving B-formatted neural representations are purely internal to the brain and, as Shapiro (2014) suggests, they could just as well be thought to occupy a well-equipped vat. The reference here is to a well-known thought experiment, the brain in the vat, which, on one interpretation, proposes to show that cognitive function, experience, and representational content would be the same for a disembodied brain in a vat, kept alive by chemicals and provided with the appropriate inputs (via direct neural stimulation), as for a fully embodied subject. Goldman introduces one careful qualification to this sort of claim; namely, that it is "possible (indeed, likely)" that the contents of such representations will depend on what they "causally interact with . . . . Envatted brain states would not have the same contents as brain states of ordinary embodied brains" (2014: 104). Body and environment may thus have some minimal role to play in this.

What precisely are B-formatted representations? Goldman (2012) admits that, despite frequent mentions of representational formats in cognitive science, it is not clear what a format is. Representations are classically thought to involve language-like (propositional) aspects, following distinctive syntactical procedures or rules that may differ across different sensory modalities (Jackendoff 2002). B-formats, however, are nonpropositional, and specifically they "represent states of the subject's own body, indeed, represent them from an internal perspective" (Goldman 2012: 73). Jesse Prinz suggests that "such representations and processes come in two forms: there are representations and processes that represent or respond to the body, such as a perception of bodily movement, and there are representations and processes that affect the body, such as motor commands" (Prinz 2009: 420). Goldman suggests that mirror neurons (activated when the perceiving subject engages in intentional action, and when the perceiver sees another agent engaged in such action) form B-formatted representations. Somatosensory, affective, and interoceptive representations are also B-formatted, "associated with the physiological conditions of the body, such as pain, temperature, itch, muscular and visceral sensations, vasomotor activity, hunger and thirst" (Goldman & de Vignemont 2009: 156). Accordingly, representations associated with an interoceptive process or motor task, where the contents of the representation are "of one's own bodily states and activities," are B-formatted and may involve proprioceptive and kinesthetic information about one's own muscles, joints, and limb positions (Goldman 2012: 71). Such information, which may originate peripherally, is B-formatted only when represented centrally: "for example, codes associated with activations in somatosensory cortex and motor cortex" (2012: 74).

In order to expand the explanatory scope of B-formats beyond cognitive operations that concern only bodily processes, Goldman adopts Michael Anderson's (2010) "reuse hypothesis"; that is, the idea that, within an evolutionary time frame, neural circuits originally established for one use can be reused or redeployed for other purposes while still maintaining their original function. For example, mirror neurons start out as motor neurons involved in motor control, but through the course of evolution they get exapted and are put to work in contexts of social cognition – activated not just for motor control, but also when one agent sees another agent act. Any cognitive task that employs a B-formatted representation, in either its original function or its exapted/ derived function is, on this definition, a form of EC.

Goldman provides some good examples of the reuse principle in linguistics. Pulvermüller's (2005) language-grounding hypothesis shows that language comprehension involves the activation of cortical motor areas. For example, when a subject hears the word *lick*, the sensorimotor area for tongue movement is activated; action words like *pick* and *kick* activate cortical areas that involve the hand and the foot, respectively. Language comprehension thus reflects the reuse of interoceptive, B-formatted motor representations. This suggests that "higher-order thought is grounded in low-level representations of motor action" (Goldman 2014: 97). In this regard, Goldman also references work by Glenberg (2010), Barsalou (1999), and Lakoff and Johnson (1999), showing how, by simulation or metaphor respectively, one can explain the embodied roots of abstract thought. Memory, for example, can involve activation of motor-control circuits (Casasanto & Dijkstra 2010); counting involves activation of motor areas related to the hand (Andres, Seron, & Olivier 2007). Accordingly, these cognitive activities should be considered as instances of EC.

Goldman also holds that B-formatted representations play some role in perception. He references the work of Dennis Proffitt, who shows that bodily states (fatigue, physical fitness), anticipation of bodily effort, and even perception of one's own body can modulate perceptual estimations of the distance, slope, and size of objects in the environment (Proffitt 2006; Proffitt et al. 1995). According to weak EC, the brain, which monitors such bodily processes, integrates perceptual information with B-formatted representations, understood as internal motor simulations, which, in turn, inform perceptual judgments about distance, slope, size, and so on. If the perceiver is fatigued or if task A will take more effort than task B, distance to target will seem longer, judged "from an 'actional' perspective" (Goldman 2012: 83).

> The subject tries to reenact the cognitive activity that would accompany the motor activity in question – without actually setting any effectors in motion. During this series of steps – or perhaps at the end – the energetic or physiological states of the system are monitored. Distance judgments are arrived at partly as a function of the detected levels of these states. (2012: 83)

Neither Proffitt nor Goldman provide details about the internal mechanisms involved, but they are characterized as a simulation process. The brain's simulation detects the levels of energy required for the task, informing perceptual judgment. Details aside, Goldman's point is that this type of process exemplifies neural reuse where B-formatted representations are redeployed for various cognitive tasks, in this case, distance perception.

From the perspective of strong embodiment – or EC more generally – this version of weak EC, which promotes the role of "sanitized" B-representations, is problematic and, paradoxically, disembodied, especially if one defines the body as not including the brain. "Embodiment theorists want to elevate the importance of the body in explaining cognitive activities. What is meant by 'body' here? It ought to mean: the whole physical body minus the brain. Letting the brain qualify as part of the body would trivialize the claim that the body is crucial to mental life" (Goldman & de Vignemont 2009: 154). In addition, weak EC removes the body from the environment in order to focus on "the body (understood literally), not [as it is related] to the situation or environment in which the body is embedded" (154). A core claim in other versions of EC, however, is that the body cannot be uncoupled from its environment. As Randall Beer (2000) puts it: "Given that bodies and nervous systems co-evolve with their environments, and only the behavior of complete animals is subjected to selection, the need for ... a tightly coupled perspective should not be surprising" (also see Brooks 1991; Chemero 2009, Chiel & Beer 1997). Without a brain, and without an environment, the literal body would be literally dead.

As Alsmith and de Vignemont point out, ideas found in weak EC "are but a hair's breadth away from the ... neurocentric idea that cognitive states are exclusively realized in neural hardware" (2012: 5). Indeed, weak EC is not inconsistent with a classic cognitivist (CC) framework. Insofar as it precludes any significant contribution from the body, it ignores the fact that EC more generally challenges this very framework. As Alsmith and Vignemont (2012: 2) acknowledge, "positing body representations actually undermines the explanatory role of the body, in the same manner in which positing representations of the world has been thought to undermine the explanatory role of the environment." They contrast this to a stronger view that "certain types of representation are so closely dependent upon the non-neural body (i.e., the body besides the brain), that their involvement in a cognitive task implicates the non-neural body itself." The fact that weak EC rejects the latter alternative is clear in Barsalou's claim that cognition operates on reactivation of motor areas, but "can indeed proceed independently of the specific body that encoded the sensorimotor experience" (2008: 619).

Let's now apply Goldman and de Vignemont's challenge questions to their own version of weak EC.

1. *Which notion of embodiment is operative?* Weak EC suggests a minimal interpretation which reduces relevant body-related processes to sanitized brain representations.

2. *Which sectors of cognition, or which cognitive tasks, are embodied; and how fully does each task involve embodiment?* Goldman and de Vignemont (2009: 158) focus on social cognition and suggest that EC is unlikely to generalize beyond that. Once Goldman (2012) adopts the reuse hypothesis, however, he thinks EC can generalize and accordingly, can be extended to a large number of cognitive operations, encompassing interoception, perception, and even higher-order processes.

3. *What empirical evidence supports specific embodiment claims?* Empirical evidence tied to research on mirror neurons, and evidence that lesions affecting B-formatted representations "interfere with action and emotion recognition," support the claims of weak EC (Goldman & de Vignemont 2009: 156). Goldman (2012; 2014) adds empirical evidence from studies by Pulvermüller, Barsalou, Proffitt, and others.

4. *How do the proffered claims depart substantially from CC?* Although weak EC seems relatively consistent with CC, the latter never anticipated the "low-level nature" of B-representations.

5. *What* role *do mental or neural representations play in cognition?* Weak EC is strongly representational. Simulations just are representations, albeit of the B-formatted kind.

3.2 Embodied Semantics

Although Goldman includes the work of Lakoff and Johnson as an example of weak EC, I'll argue that, to the extent they eschew representationalism, they occupy an intermediate position between weak EC and strong EC. According to this intermediate position, not only do the structure, composition, and motor abilities of the body determine how we experience things; they also determine what we experience, and how we understand the world. Lakoff and Johnson – drawing primarily on cognitive and experimental linguistics but also cultural anthropology, psychological, neuroscientific, and cognitive science research on mental rotation, mental imagery, gestures, and sign language – have famously argued that our conceptual life begins in spatial and motor behaviors and derives meaning from bodily experience. Accordingly, the "peculiar nature of our bodies shapes our very possibilities for conceptualization and categorization" (Lakoff & Johnson 1999: 19). For them, the specific mechanism that bridges embodied experience and conceptual thought is metaphor.

Metaphors are built on basic and recurring "image-schemas" such as front–back, in–out, near–far, pushing, pulling, supporting, balance, and so on. Basic image-schemas are, in turn, generated in bodily experience (Lakoff & Johnson 1999: 36). Thus, "the concepts of *front* and *back* are body-based. They make sense only for beings with fronts and backs. If all beings on this planet were uniform stationary spheres floating in some medium and perceiving equally in all directions, they would have no concepts of *front* and *back*" (34). Similar things can be said for *up–down, inside–outside*, and so forth. These basic image-schemas then shape, metaphorically, our abstract conceptual thought, as well as our planning and decision-making. The abstract concept of justice, for example, is characterized as a kind of balance; virtue is conceived in terms of being upright, and planning for the future is conceived in terms of up and forward – "What's coming up this week?" The *in–out* image-schema and the containment metaphor, for example, range over a vast set of concepts, from the close-to-literal – "John went out of the room" – to the abstract – "she finally came out of her depression," or "I don't want to leave any relevant data out of my argument" – to the logically abstract, such as the law of the excluded middle (Johnson 1987). This view has been extended to explanations of mathematical concepts as well (Lakoff & Núñez 2000).

On the one hand, Lakoff and Johnson endorse some forms of neural simulation. "An embodied concept is a neural structure that is part of, or makes use of the sensorimotor system of our brains. Much of conceptual inference is, therefore, sensorimotor inference" (Lakoff & Johnson 1999: 20). The Lakoff–Johnson view may also be consistent with a connectionist view, and on one interpretation (Zlatev 2010) it is not inconsistent with classic cognitivism. Yet, the fact that Lakoff and Johnson eschew internal representations moves them closer to strong, even enactivist views of EC.

> As we said in *Philosophy in the Flesh*, the only workable theory of representations is one in which a representation is a flexible pattern of organism-environment interactions, and not some inner mental entity that somehow gets hooked up with parts of the external world by a strange relation called "reference." We reject such classic notions of representation, along with the views of meaning and reference that are built on them. Representation is a term that we try carefully to avoid. (Johnson & Lakoff 2002: 249–250)

3.3 Strong EC

In contrast to weak EC, which denies that anatomy and bodily movement are important factors for cognition, strong EC suggests that anatomy and movement are nontrivial contributors to the shaping of cognition prior to brain processing (preprocessing) and subsequent to brain processing (postprocessing) (e.g., Chiel & Beer 1997; Shapiro 2004). Embodiment in this case means that extra-neural structural features of the body shape our cognitive experience (Gallagher 2005a). For example, the fact that we have two eyes, positioned as they are, delivers us binocular vision and allows us to see the relative depth of things. Similar observations can be made about the position of our ears and our ability to tell the direction of sound. As Shapiro puts it, "the point is not simply [or trivially] that perceptual processes fit bodily structure. Perceptual processes *depend on and include* bodily structures" (2004: 190).

Our sensory experiences also depend on the way our heads and bodies move, as we see in the case of perceptual parallax displacement (Churchland, Ramachandran, & Sejnowski 1994). Furthermore, our motor responses, rather than being fully determined at brain level, are mediated by the design of muscles and tendons, their degrees of flexibility, their geometric relationships to other muscles and joints, their complex degrees of freedom, and their prior history of activation (Berthoz 2000). This sort of evidence motivates the idea that movement is not always centrally planned; it is based on a competitive system that requires what Andy Clark terms "soft assembly." The nervous system learns "to modulate parameters (such as stiffness [of limb or joint]) which will then *interact* with intrinsic bodily and environmental constraints so as to yield desired outcomes" (Clark 1997: 45).

The claims of strong EC are also based on the following kinds of evidence. Various experiments show that how we are moving or posturing ourselves (e.g., pushing something away from our body versus pulling something toward it) will affect our evaluations of target objects (e.g., Chen & Bargh 1999). Likewise, in experiments by Glenberg and Kaschak (2002), subjects pressed a button or pulled a lever to indicate whether action sentences made sense or not – for example, sentences like "open the drawer" (which involves a pulling toward the body) or "close the drawer" (which involves pushing away from the body). Reaction times were shorter when the response motion was in the same direction as the motion represented by the action sentences (see Varga 2018 for a review of other experiments like this).

As Shapiro notes: "steps in a cognitive process that a traditionalist would attribute to symbol manipulation might, from the perspective of [strong] EC, emerge from the physical attributes of the body" (2007: 340). Still, many of these results are cast in terms of information processing, and in that respect may be construed as consistent with the general principles of classic cognitivism. Even if the body is doing some of the work, cognitivists could easily claim that preprocessing is in fact feeding the central processing that is truly constitutive of cognition, just as postprocessing is to some degree determined by instructions from the brain as central processor.

More holistic, biological, proprioceptive, and emotion-related processes, however, may be more challenging to the classic conception. There is long-standing empirical evidence that such processes have a profound effect on perception and thinking. For example, vibration-induced proprioceptive patterns that change the posture of the whole body are interpreted as changes in the perceived environment (Roll & Roll 1988), while postural-proprioceptive adjustments of the body can help to resolve perceptual conflicts (Rock & Harris 1967). Alterations of the postural schema (e.g., subsequent to bariatric surgery) can lead to alterations in space perception (Natvik et al. 2019). Likewise, hormonal changes – changes in body chemistry – as well as visceral and musculoskeletal processes can bias perception, memory, attention, and decision-making (Damasio 1994; Gallagher 2005a; Shapiro 2004). The regulation of body chemistry is not autonomous of cognitive processes, and vice versa. "Body regulation, survival, and mind are intimately interwoven" (Damasio 1994: 123).

Accordingly, it's not just proprioceptive or motoric processes that play into cognitive processing. In this respect one notes the importance of pervasive affective processes, which include emotion and mood, but also basic bodily processes that pertain to hunger, fatigue, and hedonic sensations. Somaesthetic factors such as hunger or fatigue delimit our perception and action possibilities, as well as our cognitive processes. A study by Danziger, Levav, and Avnaim-Pesso (2011), for example, reinforces the idea that hunger can shape, and perhaps even distort, cognitive processes. Judicial decisions in a court of law are not simply a matter of the rational application of legal reasons. Whether the judge is hungry or satiated may play an important role. "The percentage of favorable rulings drops gradually from ≈65% to nearly zero within each decision session [e.g., between breakfast and lunch] and returns abruptly to ≈65% after a [food] break. Our findings suggest that judicial rulings can be swayed by extraneous variables that should have no bearing on legal decisions" (Danziger et al. 2011: 1). In one sense, such affective factors appear "extraneous" only if we think of cognition as disembodied, although clearly they may be considered extraneous to the formal aspects of legal reasoning. Still, hunger can have an effect on the jurist's perception of the facts, as well as on the weighing of evidence (see Varga [2018] for the implications of EC for courtroom interactions and for challenges to juridical legitimacy).

The experiments by Proffitt, cited by Goldman in support of weak EC can be interpreted as supporting a stronger version of EC. Proffitt et al. (1995) show that fatigue, or more directly, physical burden, for example, can affect perception; subjects estimate the grade of an incline to be steeper while wearing a heavy backpack in comparison to when they are wearing none. Typically, however, this would not be a simple, isolated effect based on a single isolated affective state. Rather, we typically experience a mélange of affective processes. My trek up the mountain results in a perception of the path in front of me that is informed by a combination of my fatigue, my troubled respiration, my hunger, my pain, my feelings of dirtiness, and the kinesthetic difficulty involved in climbing. More generally, the mountain path looks quite different and less challenging after a good night's sleep, not because the objective qualities of the path have changed but because of my affective state. As such, affective processes may manifest themselves in the impact they have on perception and action without me knowing it (i.e., prenoetically), despite modulating my phenomenal consciousness.

Affective factors thus involve a complex motivational dimension that animates body–world interaction (Colombetti 2014; Stapleton 2013;). Affect is deeply embodied. It is constrained by the functioning of the circulatory system, for example. Heartbeat influences how and whether fear-inducing stimuli (e.g., images of fearful faces presented to experimental subjects) are processed (Garfinkel et al. 2014). When the heart contracts in its systole phase, fearful stimuli are more easily recognized, and they tend to be perceived as more fearful than when presented in its diastole phase. Likewise, experiments on respiration show significant modulations on cognitive processes, including emotion and pain perception, with variations in breathing (Varga & Heck 2017; Zelano et al. 2016). Noting the importance of such embodied factors gives us a perspective that can breathe life into the strong EC account. The fact that we are flesh-and-blood creatures, living bodies equipped with beating hearts, rather than brains in vats, explains in part why we have just the sorts of affective states and perceptual experiences that we do.

Strong EC thus requires that we acknowledge the role of core bio-systemic processes that range across motoric, interoceptive, affective, autonomic, endocrine, and enteric functions. On this reading of EC, the classic thought experiment of the brain in the vat is unworkable because it fails to take into consideration the contributions of body performances. As several theorists have pointed out, the vat engineers would have to replicate everything that the biological body delivers in terms of pre-and postprocessing, precise and time-constrained hormonal and neurotransmitter chemistry, emotional life, and so on. As Damasio suggests, this would require the creation of a body surrogate "and thus confirm that 'body-type inputs' are required for a normally minded brain after all" (1994: 228; also see Cosmelli & Thompson 2007; Gallagher 2005b). Note, then, that strong EC does not deny the importance of the brain. Our understanding of brain function, however, depends on the fact that the brain and the body coevolved – again, something that we have known for a long time, at least since the time at which distinctions between psychology, physiology, and philosophy were being initiated: "You must understand the living organism before you can interpret the function of the brain" (Lewes 1879: 75).

The challenge questions are:

1. *Which notion of embodiment is operative?* Strong EC suggests that the full body's neural and nonneural factors, including a good variety of bodily systems (motoric, affective, autonomic, etc.), play significant roles in cognition.

2. *Which sectors of cognition, or which cognitive tasks, are embodied, and how fully does each task involve embodiment?* According to the studies we cited, various aspects of embodiment are fully involved in perception and action but also in evaluative judgments. Later, we'll show that bodily (motoric and affective) processes play an important role in social cognition.

3. *What empirical evidence supports specific embodiment claims?* Studies of kinesthetics, motor control and body schematic processes, perceptual tracking, neural synchronization, respiration, and so on, support the idea that bodily processes play important roles in perception and judgment.

4. *How do the proffered claims depart substantially from CC?* Strong EC emphasizes the role of physical extraneural processes that are not well captured by computational models.

5. *What role do mental or neural representations play in cognition?* Strong EC tends to emphasize the role of bodily and environmental physical processes rather than internal representations. As we'll see shortly, however, this does not rule out the idea that external representations may play a significant role in learning, problem-solving, and communication.

4 The Second E: Embedded Cognition

The general idea of embedded cognition is that in some cases the environment scaffolds our cognitive processes, or that engagement with environmental features can shift cognitive load. Robert Rupert explains: "Cognitive processes depend very heavily, in hitherto unexpected ways, on organismically external props and devices and on the structure of the external environment in which cognition takes place" (2004: 393). When agents coordinate their activity with environmental resources such as external artifacts, cognitive processes may be productively constrained or enabled by objective features, or enhanced by the affordances on offer. Examples include using written notes to reduce demands on working memory, setting a timer as a reminder to do something, using a map or the surrounding landscape to assist in navigation, or – since the environment is not just physical, but also social – asking another person for directions. As Margaret Wilson put it: "rather than attempt to mentally store and manipulate all the relevant details about a situation, we physically store and manipulate those details out in the world, in the very situation itself" (2002: 629). The most straightforward claims in this regard are based on processes that are pervasive. One can think of learning and educational practices, the reliance on books, chalk- or whiteboards, the arrangement of classrooms, interaction with instructors, and so on. One can also think of how we gain knowledge in science, where passive observation is less the rule than active manipulation using instruments and labs to refine discovery and measurement, or the use of diagrams and charts to organize our conclusions. That such practices scaffold our thinking processes can be seen in cases where the use of such tools produces new knowledge. For example, drawing a diagram to demonstrate a result may lead to new realizations, new diagrams, new experiments, and new knowledge (Bredo 1994).

Under the heading of embedded cognition we can list several different approaches including situated cognition, distributed cognition, and ecological cognition. Although the term "situated cognition" is sometimes regarded as equivalent to EC more generally (Robbins & Aydede 2009), embedded cognition includes the idea that agents are actively or passively situated in the environment. On the one hand, situated agents can engage in "epistemic actions" – actions that actively manipulate the environment to reduce cognitive load (Kirsh & Maglio 1994). On the other hand, situated cognition may mean that the environment plays a constraining or enabling role. In this regard, context matters; physical, social, and cultural contexts may make specific forms of cognition possible. Certain environments may facilitate cognition and learning, while other environments don't. Embedded/situated cognition allows for the possibility that a specific design or rearrangement of an environment, including virtual (computer-simulated) environments, can facilitate learning and problem-solving. The concept of cognitive niche construction, which originates in the field of biological evolution, is relevant here (Sterelny 2010) and is also developed in extended mind contexts (Clark 2008a; Wheeler & Clark 2008). On this view, organisms (and species) improve their chances of survival and their ability to solve problems by modifying their environments, or actively transforming long-term relations with the environment. Philosophically, the common message is that cognition does not happen in thin air, or abstractly in-the-head, but is always, as a phenomenologist might say, in-the-world, or as Edwin Hutchins might say, "in the wild."

Hutchins is known for his work in the area of distributed cognition, which is committed to the idea that the boundaries and mechanisms of the cognitive system may be distributed in the sense that they may involve (1) coordination between internal and external (material or environmental) structures; (2) processes distributed across time, such that products of earlier events can transform later events; and (3) the coordinated efforts of members of a team, including artificial agents (Hutchins 2000). He develops this idea in his analysis of ship navigation (Hutchins 1995a). Navigators solve cognitively complex problems (e.g., calculating the speed of the ship in knots) by working together and using instruments (such as nomogram and a straight-edge ruler).

> It is clear that cognitive work is being done, but it is also clear that the processes inside the person are not, by themselves, sufficient to accomplish the computation. A larger unit of analysis must be considered. The skills of scale reading and interpolation are coordinated with the manipulation of objects to establish a particular state of coordination between the straightedge and the nomogram. (Hutchins 2000: 8)

The solution to the problem, the calculation, is achieved by the manipulation of the artifact, which is something that allows for a more reliable result than attempting to work it out in one's head, or even by pencil and paper. Cognitive work can be accomplished by engaging with collaborative technologies which support the productive interaction of team members (who play different roles). In the context of team cognition this has often been framed in terms of shared external representations, which may be communicated in whole or in part by various media, examples of which can be found not only in navigational systems of naval vessels, but in airline cockpits (Hutchins 1995b), and air-traffic control systems (Halverson 1995). In such contexts we find cognitive artifacts that not only augment existing human capabilities, but transform the task into a different one, "allowing resources to be reallocated into a configuration that better suits the cognitive capabilities of the problem solver," even when that problem solver is a team rather than an individual (Perry 2003: 201; Fiore et al. 2003).

The ecological approach, deriving from James Gibson's ecological psychology, starts, "in the wild," with our natural and constructed niches, and explains how action possibilities are enabled or constrained by environmental structure. Gibson builds his ecological understanding of embodied action around the concept of affordances: "The affordances of the environment are what it offers the animal, what it provides or furnishes, either for good or ill" (1979: 127). Gibson was influenced by Merleau-Ponty (2012), who in turn carried forward the phenomenological concept of the "I can" (Husserl 1989) or "ready-to-hand" (Heidegger 1962) – the idea that we experience the world perceptually in pragmatic terms of what we can do with the objects that surround us. The term "affordance" efficiently captures these concepts. We'll have more to say about ecological views in Section 6, since they help to shape certain enactive approaches.

How does embedded cognition answer the challenge questions?

1. *Which notion of embodiment is operative?* Embedded cognition emphasizes how a perceiving and agentive body engages with the environment, and the causal role of artifacts, props, technological instruments, and so on, in cognition.

2. *Which sectors of cognition, or which cognitive tasks, are embodied; and how fully does each task involve embodiment?* Learning, memory, problem-solving, and epistemic actions more generally depend on bodily interaction with the physical and social environment.

3. *What empirical evidence supports specific embodiment claims?* Experimental psychology (including experiments in ecological psychology), studies in evolutionary science, and ethnographic studies of specific pragmatic and social contexts support a variety of claims made by embedded cognition.

4. *How do the proffered claims depart substantially from CC?* Embedded cognition emphasizes the role of body–environment interactions that are not usually considered by CC.

5. *What role do mental or neural representations play in cognition?* Most embedded cognition theorists share with strong EC an emphasis on the role of bodily and environmental physical processes rather than internal representations. Rupert (2011), however, endorses the idea of a "massively representational mind," although he conceives of representations in a minimal sense (see Section 6.2 for further discussion). Most generally, from the embedded cognition view, external representations operate as instruments that can play a role in learning, problem-solving, and communication.

5 The Third E: Extended Cognition

Both the historical background and the contemporary foreground that inform the concept of extended mind are complex. In the deep philosophical background one can find a prefiguring of the extended-mind hypothesis (EMH) in pragmatists like Charles Sanders Peirce and John Dewey. Peirce, for example, contends that "it is no figure of speech to say that the alembics and cucurbits of the chemist are instruments of thought, or logical machines" (1887: 168). He also suggests that his inkstand can count as part of his thinking apparatus.

> A psychologist cuts out a lobe of my brain . . . and then, when I find I cannot express myself, he says, "You see, your faculty of language was localized in that lobe." No doubt it was; and so, if he had filched my inkstand, I should not have been able to continue my discussion until I had got another. Yea, the very thoughts would not come to me. So my faculty of discussion is equally localized in my inkstand. (Peirce 1958: 366)

Likewise, Dewey affirms a parity between brain processes, the agent's body, and various tools and instruments in the thinking process.

> Hands and feet, apparatus and appliances of all kinds are as much a part of [thinking] as changes in the brain. Since these physical operations (including the cerebral events) and equipments are a part of thinking, thinking is mental, not because of a peculiar stuff which enters into it or of peculiar non-natural activities which constitute it, but because of what physical acts and appliances do: the distinctive purpose for which they are employed and the distinctive results which they accomplish. (Dewey 1916: 8–9)

Operating more immediately in the background are thinkers like John Haugeland (1991; 1995), who Clark (1997) draws on to work out whether and how representations fit with the EMH; Edwin Hutchins (1995a), whose notion of distributed cognition seems a close cousin to extended mind; and Rodney Brooks (1991), whose robotic designs make material structures do most of the navigational work. Extended mind is also influenced by connectionism and neural net theory.

By the contemporary foreground I mean the initial reception (or in some cases the rejection) of the EMH and its continuing development in a series of theoretical "waves" (Sutton 2010; also see Cash 2013; Kirchhoff 2012; Menary 2010a). Our starting point, however, has to be Clark and Chalmers (1998) and the formation that is sometimes called the first wave.

5.1 The First Wave

Clark and Chalmers start with a question about location: "Where does the mind stop and the rest of the world begin?" (1998: 7) – is the mind "in the head," or does it extend out into the world? A different way to frame the question is to ask, not *where* the mind is, but what we mean by the mind such that it can (or cannot) be said to extend beyond the traditional boundaries of the skull or even the body? In answering this question Clark and Chalmers propose the framework of "active externalism." On this view, the physical mechanisms (or "vehicles") that underpin cognition include not just neuronal structures, but also extraneural factors, such as instruments or artifacts in the environment.[2] By calling it "active" externalism, Clark and Chalmers mean to emphasize not just the environmental resources, but also the idea that the cognitive agent's activity (or what Kirsh and Maglio [1994] had called "epistemic action") plays an important role. Indeed, their first example is about a person who accomplishes a cognitive task by taking action, that is, by manipulating things in the environment (or in this case, while playing the game of Tetris, manipulating shapes on a computer screen). This example leads to a statement of what has become known as the *parity principle*. If in playing Tetris, a player physically manipulates the geometric shapes using a rotate button on the computer in order to figure out where they will fit, this action is said to be functionally equivalent to activating a connected neural implant to physically rotate the geometric shapes, or to mentally rotate the shapes by activating neurons. That is, these activities/ activations are doing the same job. Specifically, there is little difference between activating neurons and activating a neural implant; moreover, "if the rotation [using the neural implant] is cognitive, by what right do we count [using the rotation button] as fundamentally different?" (Clark & Chalmers 1998: 7). This leads directly to the parity principle.

> If, as we confront some task, a part of the world functions as a process which, were it done in the head, we would have no hesitation in recognizing as part of the cognitive process, then that part of the world is (so we claim) part of the cognitive process. (Clark & Chalmers 1998: 8)

Clark and Chalmers emphasize that the brain may in fact come to depend on specific types of coupling to environmental factors, but also that it may be the cognizer's capacity to couple systematically with a wide variety of elements, rather than any one specific tool or environmental factor, that is of greater importance.

There is a subtle shift in Clark and Chalmers's essay from claims about cognitive processes to claims about mental states, such as beliefs. This is accomplished in a second example, in which they demonstrate that beliefs may be constituted in part by environmental factors. This purportedly justifies a stronger claim; namely, that the mind itself extends. The second example is the story of Otto and Inga, where Otto, having some problems with his biological memory, uses a notebook where he has written down the location of a museum. The outcome, his access to his dispositional belief recorded in his notebook, is

---

[2] For the distinction between content and vehicle, see Dennett (1969: 56) and Millikan (1991). Hurley (2010) distinguishes a variety of externalisms, and associates extended mind with vehicle or "how" externalism.

said to be "on a par with" an equivalent belief generated by processes of neural-based memory in Inga's head (Clark 2010b: 86; see Wheeler 2019).

Anticipating objections to this strong parity claim, Clark and Chalmers add three further criteria, which became known as the glue-and-trust criteria (Clark 2010b: 83), to be met by external factors if they are to be included as part of the cognitive system: reliability, trustworthiness, and accessibility.

1. That the external resource be reliably available and typically invoked.
2. That any information thus retrieved be more-or-less automatically endorsed. It should not usually be subject to critical scrutiny (unlike the opinions of other people, for example). It should be deemed about as trustworthy as something retrieved clearly from biological memory.
3. That information contained in the resource should be easily accessible as and when required (Clark 2008a: 79).

The first critics of the EMH were not appeased by these criteria. They raised three main objections. The first, and perhaps easiest to answer, is the *cognitive bloat* objection (Rupert 2004; Rowlands 2009). The EMH runs the risk of extending cognition too far beyond the traditional notion of cognition, to include all kinds of technologies (smartphones, the internet, etc.) as part of the mind. Would we really want to call processes happening in the circuits of my iPhone or the Google search engine part of my cognitive system? One response to this worry is simply to reiterate the three criteria we have already mentioned. If we accept the criteria of reliability, trustworthiness, and accessibility, they seemingly put the brakes on how far we can go in this direction. Perhaps a better response, however, is to emphasize the active aspect of active externalism. Cognition consists of a manipulation by an agent, and the kinds of action that couple in the right way to the world – namely couplings that involve reciprocal causal relations where outputs are recycled as inputs (Clark 2008a: 131). Cognition reaches only as far as this coupling reaches, and without this coupling there is no claim that cognition extends. This does place real limitations on what counts as cognitive. We'll return to this point in Section 6.

A second objection concerning *the mark of the mental* is raised by Adams and Aizawa (2001: 48) who contend, from the perspective of CC, that only processes that involve intrinsic, nonderived intentional (representational) content can be considered cognitive. Intrinsic content, they claim, is neurally generated in internal representational processes; as such, it just is the mark of the mental. In contrast, the manipulation of external factors involves no intrinsic content outside of the brain. Although Clark (2010b) responds by arguing that a mix of intrinsic content with other nonintrinsic resources constitutes cognitive states, one might also think that the issue should not be about content, but about the processes (or vehicles) that generate or carry content. The question is whether such processes are exclusively neuronal or can include processes such as language use, writing in notebooks, or epistemic actions. Clark interprets this in a functionalist way that may be construed as consistent with CC. That is, an element is part of a cognitive system based on its function, or the type of coupling it is capable of, and it is just this which makes it "a candidate for becoming a proper part of a genuinely cognitive process" (2010b: 85).[3]

> Then what settles the question of whether that part belongs to this cognitive system, or to that one, or (currently) to no cognitive system at all? It is hard to see just what, apart from appeal to some kind of coupling, at some time in the causal-historical chain, could motivate an answer to this subsequent question. (Clark 2010b: 85)

On a functionalist view, no element or process is *intrinsically* cognitive – neither neuronal processes nor the use of a notebook – it is only cognitive in terms of the role it plays in the system as a whole. In this respect, Menary (2010b), from the EC perspective, suggests that the insistence on intrinsic or representational content leads to an impoverished concept of cognition.

A third objection concerns the *causal coupling-constitution (C-C) fallacy*. This objection zeroes in on the main difference between embedded cognition and extended cognition. Adams and Aizawa (2001) claim that the EMH confuses causality (or coupling) with constitution. In their view, Otto's use of, or coupling with his notebook involves a causal relation or enabling condition. On an embedded cognition view, the notebook can support or scaffold Otto's cognition, but it cannot constitute cognition, in the sense of being an operative part of the cognition process. Clark and Chalmers seemingly ignore the distinction between causality and constitution. Their claim starts as a functionalist causal one: "[a]ll the components [whether neural or extraneural] in the system play an active causal role" (1998: 12). Accordingly, if neural processes, as causal vehicles, constitute cognition, so do extraneural processes if they play an equivalent causal role. In some way, however, this nontrivial causality adds up to constitution. Adams and Aizawa's objection, in contrast, is based on a strict distinction between causality and constitution. Since this objection counts equally as an objection to claims made by enactive approaches, we'll forego resolving it here, and return to discuss the C-C fallacy in Section 7.1.

---

[3] For detailed discussion of the relationship between functionalism and the extended mind, see Sprevak (2009); Miyazono (2017); and Wadham (2016).

5.2 The Second Wave

A number of theorists who endorse the idea of the extended mind nonetheless have raised some friendly criticisms. Some of these criticisms, and some of the solutions, were anticipated by Clark and Chalmers – specifically concerning notions of activity, complementarity, and social extension. From the perspective of the second-wave theorists, however, the main problem with the original version of the EMH concerns the parity principle. Clark (2008a) and Michael Wheeler (2012) defend the parity principle, complemented by the three criteria of reliability, trustworthiness, and accessibility. According to them, the parity principle should not be interpreted as requiring anything like a similarity between inner and outer processes; rather, we should read the principle in functionalist terms, and as stating a sufficient rather than a necessary condition.

Second-wave theorists, however, view the parity principle as a clandestine Cartesian supposition, such that internal processes are to be the measure of what counts as cognitive. John Sutton (2010) argues that cutting ties to the parity principle is not to deny that in some cases there may be a functional similarity between inner and outer processes, but there are also many significant differences. This can be seen in a variety of ways, including in Hutchins' (1995a, 1995b) research on distributed cognition where heterogeneous resources are integrated to accomplish cognitive tasks. In contrast to parity, Sutton defends complementarity, which includes the idea that "different components of the overall (enduring or temporary) system can play quite different [functional] roles and have different properties while coupling in collective and complementary contributions to flexible thinking and acting" (Sutton 2010: 194). Degrees of complementarity vary across different cognizers and differences in particular environments. Individual agents may use different proportions of external props and instruments *versus* internal processes like memorization, and the proportions might alter from day to day, situation to situation, as much as from person to person, as well as across changes or different structures in the environment. Clark and Chalmers (1998) can easily endorse this view, since they already suggested that the brain can develop "in a way that complements the external structures" (12); and that an external resource such as language is "not a mirror of our inner states but a complement to them" (18). The second wave refocuses on these ideas. Sutton (2010: 204), drawing on research in distributed cognition, argues that "the various nonhuman artifacts which scaffold successful performance" (or what Clark [1997: 77] had called a "heterogeneous assembly") do not "have to be doing the same thing as the individual participants are, or even storing the same information as might have been stored in their individual brains."

Richard Menary (2007; 2010b) emphasizes the second-wave theme of integration. Integration, in contrast to embeddedness or mere scaffolding, is predicated on reciprocal causal connections activated by active bodily manipulations of the environment, a form of active coupling. Bodily manipulations involve sensory-motor processes that shape, and are shaped by, the specifics of physical and social environments. According to Menary, such manipulations include, besides the *epistemic actions* mentioned above, *biological couplings*, described in terms of sensory-motor contingencies by O'Regan and Noë (2001), *self-correcting actions*, that is, the use of language, props, and tools to guide completion of tasks, and *cognitive practices*. Menary develops the latter in greater detail; they involve "the manipulation of external representational and notational systems according to certain normative practices – as in mathematics" (2010b: 237). Numbers, diagrams, drawings, maps, charts, and so on are external representations that allow us to accomplish cognitive tasks. We manipulate such things using pencils and paper, computers, and reorganizing spatial arrangements, and we do so following norms that are culturally established and learned. These practices are integrated with the internal activities of our brains and mediated by the movements of our bodies. On this view, this kind of integration involves not a simple offloading or scaffolding that simplifies cognition, but a transformation of cognitive processes such that we can think and act in new ways through such engagements.

One good example of a cognitive practice is writing.

> Stable and enduring external written sentences allow for manipulation, transformations, reorderings, comparisons, and deletions of text that are not available to neural processes. This is the upshot of second-wave cognitive-integration-style arguments: bodily manipulations of external vehicles are different from, but complementary to, internal processes. (Menary 2010b: 240)

In contrast to claims about embedded scaffolding, then, integration is not a one-way, agent-, or brain-to-world relation. Rather, through our engagements with tools and artifacts, our brains undergo plastic changes over evolutionary and developmental timeframes. A world-to-agent relation is captured by a version of the EMH that emphasizes what our engagement with the material world does to us. It changes our practices and our brains. Not only our causal interactions with the material aspects of our environment over time, but also our cultural practices, as we engage with social and normative aspects of our surrounding world, result in an integrated metaplasticity, that is, a set of correlated changes in brains, practices, and environments (Malafouris 2013). In this respect, the properties of the "internal" and the "external" are not fixed (Kirchhoff 2012). Specifically in cases of writing and communication, the development of different media already shows how the material we use not only enables cognition, but transforms the very nature of cognition, the possibilities of joint action and, importantly, our communicative practices.

This point about communicative practices leads to the idea of the *socially* extended mind. Again, Clark and Chalmers (1998: 17–18) had anticipated this idea in suggesting that "my mental states might be partly constituted by the mental states of other thinkers .... one's beliefs might be embodied in one's secretary, one's accountant, or one's collaborator." In this respect cognition extends across social dyads, teams, or small groups where coupling is often direct, active, and mutual. The notion of the socially extended mind, however, takes this idea further. It suggests that just such practices allow for the establishment of what I've called mental or cognitive institutions (Gallagher 2013). In this respect, extended mind is not just about the use of handheld notebooks, iPhones, writing tablets, diagrams, maps, and so on. It's also about the use of, or engagement with large-scale institutions, for example, academic, scientific, legal, and cultural institutions that enable cognition, and, indeed, as we engage with them, even constitute specific types of cognitive accomplishments. The legal institution is a good example of a set of structures and practices that includes normatively defined cognitive practices. Institutions like the legal system, when we engage with them (that is, when we interact with, or are coupled to them in the right way), are activated in ways that extend our cognitive processes and help us to solve problems of a particular type. Legal contracts, for example, embody conceptual schemas that contribute to and shape some of our cognitive practices. They are themselves products of specific cognitive exercises, but they are also used as tools to accomplish certain aims, to reinforce behavior, and to solve problems. They operate as such, however, only in the context of a larger and more complex legal institution. Accordingly, institutions, and the precise way that we use them, not only constrain our thinking about social arrangements, and about acceptable behavior, but allow us to think in ways that would not otherwise be possible.

In some instances of the socially extended mind, the glue-and-trust criteria may be important, but they do not always or necessarily rule. The legal system, for example, may not be reliably available or easily accessible (this may be a matter of degree and dependent on issues that involve things like social or immigration status, or racist practices). When we do engage with it, however, it can sometimes support and add stability to our decisions or judgments. Likewise, the kind of critical scrutiny intrinsic to legal proceedings is a kind of justified mistrust, which itself involves a reflective cognitive process, and should not disqualify the overall process from being an instance of extended cognition.

5.3 The Third Wave

Waves are not always well formed. That sometimes makes them difficult to count. This is especially true when the latest wave is still in the formation process. Accordingly, there are different opinions about where the second wave stops and the third wave commences. Michael Kirchhoff (2012), for example, suggests that the third wave consists of an emphasis on the dynamical meta-plasticity of the relation between internal and external, and he lists the socially extended mind (the concept of cognitive institutions), which I have mentioned as part of the second wave, as a good example. Mason Cash (2013), in relatively close agreement, also takes the third wave to be based on the socially extended mind. Fritzman and Thornburg (2016) define the socially extended mind as a fourth wave. How we count these things may be somewhat arbitrary at this point. For our purposes here, I will suggest that the third wave is less continuous than the first and second, and it introduces some new complicating considerations about predictive processing (PP) and how extended cognition is related to enactive approaches. In this regard, the third wave points us toward the fourth E, enactive cognition (which we take up in Section 6). To finish our discussion here, however, we need to consider a debate within PP accounts of cognition that mirrors the difference (or, as the case may be, the continuity) between CC and EC.

One worry that haunts the first two waves of extended mind is a concern about what it means to do cognitive science if one is forced to study such a heterogeneous collection of factors: neurons, notebooks, diagrams, iPhones, legal institutions, and so on. Such a set of cognitive elements "would seem to form such a motley collection that they will not form the basis of any significant scientific theorizing" (Adams & Aizawa 2001: 63). This challenge motivates the desire, among some proponents of the extended mind, to find a more unified scientific approach. Is there some way that cognitive science could integrate all of these different factors within a unified explanatory model? This seems to be precisely what a PP approach promises, as evidenced in the continuing work of Clark (2016) and his project of linking PP and extended mind.

More immediately, however, we should consider whether PP can find a place within the general framework of EC.

The connection between extended mind and PP runs through Clark's recent work, and specifically his book *Surfing Uncertainty* (2016). His version of PP, however, contrasts with the internalist, neurocentric versions, as found in Jakob Hohwy (2013), for example. The question, then, is whether a fully embodied and extended version of PP is possible.

Predictive processing has been promoted as an approach to neuroscience that explains how the brain works in all of its functional aspects. Predictive processing continues a long tradition, going back to Helmholtz (1962/1867), which understands perception as an inferential process. It models this process in terms of prediction error minimization (PEM), which begins with the assumption that the brain lacks access to the external world.

> [The brain] must discover information about the likely causes of impinging signals without any form of direct access to their source .... [A]ll that it "knows," in any direct sense, are the ways its own states (e.g., spike trains) flow and alter. In that (restricted) sense, all the system has direct access to is its own states. The world itself is thus off-limits. (Clark 2013: 183)

By means of perceptual inference, neuronal processes represent the world by forming a set of hierarchically arranged probabilistic hypotheses about it based on an internal Bayesian (statistical) generative model that it constructs informed by prior knowledge (priors). The prediction structure can be quite complex, involving a nested cascade of precision-weighted predictive processes in the brain. The brain's task is to take "patterns of neural activation and, on that basis alone, infer properties of the stimulus" (Clark 2016). When the brain receives specific sensory input, it treats it as evidence that either confirms or disconfirms its hypotheses. If there is a significant mismatch between its predictions and the sensory input, the brain revises its model and corrects its inferences in order to minimize prediction errors.

> The human brain, PP here suggests, commands a rich, integrated model of the worldly sources of sensory inputs, and uses that long-term model to generate on-the-spot predictions about the probable shape and character of current inputs. The rich, integrated (generative) model takes a highly distributed form, spread across multiple neural areas that may communicate in complex context-varying manners. (Clark 2018: 522)

Once the brain generates a prediction that comes close to or matches the sensory input, it has a good grasp on the world. This grasp will be immediately challenged as things change and new prediction errors are generated.

The system can follow a different strategy, however, a process termed "active inference." In contrast to perceptual inference, active inference maintains its current model and engages in action that changes the environment, thereby changing its sensory input to reduce prediction error.

> [Active] "inference," as it functions in the [PP] story, is not compelled to deliver internal states that bear richly reconstructive contents. It is not there to construct an inner realm able to stand in for the full richness of the external world. Instead, it may deliver efficient, low-cost strategies whose unfolding

and success depend delicately and continuously upon the structure and ongoing contributions of the external realm itself as exploited by various forms of action and intervention. (Clark 2016: 191)

There are a lot more technical details to the PP story; for example, that the system's predictions are based on Bayesian probability; that it is organized in layers of hierarchical processing with each layer attempting to predict activation of the level below it; and that there is a recursive reliability function that bestows different precision weights on predictions (i.e., how probable they are).

Accounts of cognition based on PEM are typically framed in narrow, internalist terms where all of the important action is to be found in brain processes, reflecting a strict boundary between brain and world (defined in mathematical terms by a formalism termed a Markov blanket; see Friston 2013). Hohwy (2013) shows how this kind of account can work as a strictly internalist explanation of what the brain does, given that it has no direct access to the external environment. It deals only with sensory inputs, or it employs active inference to change those inputs. For Hohwy, PEM is primary; active inference is in service to the central processes that do the real work. To that extent, bodily, ecological, or environmental factors seem irrelevant to explaining cognition.

> PEM should make us resist conceptions of [a mind–world] relation on which the mind is in some fundamental way open or porous to the world, or on which it is in some strong sense embodied, extended or enactive. Instead, PEM reveals the mind to be inferentially secluded from the world, it seems to be more neurocentrically skull-bound than embodied or extended, and action itself is more an inferential process on sensory input than an enactive coupling with the environment. (Hohwy 2016: 259)

On such an account, at best, the body plays the role of sensory information source in a process where descending predictions from the brain are compared with ascending prediction errors from the sensory periphery in an inferential process by which the brain models the world.

Clark, however, offers a more optimistic view concerning EC, and especially the perspectives of extended, and perhaps even enactive cognition. "PP thus provides, or so I will argue, the perfect neuro-computational partner for recent work on the embodied mind – work that stresses the constant engagement of the world by cycles of perceptual-motor activity" (2016: 1). In effect, Clark, in contrast to Hohwy, emphasizes active inference – active, embodied engagement that manipulates the environment in order to reduce prediction errors. "The predictive brain, if this is correct, is not an insulated inference engine so much as an action-oriented engagement machine" (Clark 2016: 1).

The important thing about active inference is that it is not just a tool that the brain might use to test or sample the environment, although this is often the way that it is portrayed: a process of "sampling the world in ways designed to test our hypotheses and to yield better information for the control of action itself" (Clark 2016: 7, 290). That would be consistent with Hohwy's interpretation (see Hohwy 2013: 79). Rather, for Clark, active inference should be conceived as involving the agent's constant world-enacting movement, the kind of action that modulates the structure of the agent's social and material environment. Thus, "[o]ur neural economy exists to serve the needs of embodied action" (2016: 269), rather than the other way around.

> Such world-structuring, repeated time and time again, generation by gener-
> ation, also enables beings like us to build better and better worlds to think in,
> allowing impinging energies to guide ever-more-complex forms of behavior
> and enabling thought and reason to penetrate domains that were previously
> "off-limits." (2016: 7)

Specifically, as Clark suggests (2016: 275ff), we can minimize prediction errors by designing our environments to be more cognition friendly. Predictive procesing, in emphasizing active inference, allows for the "integration" (2016: 9) of the complementary aspects of brain–body–environment sought in the second wave of extended mind.

Clark describes these integration processes as "rolling cycles" in which "what we perceive is constantly conditioned by what we do." In an ongoing reciprocal causal fashion, top-down predictions entrain actions that "help sculpt the sensory flows that recruit new high-level predictions (and so on, in a rolling cycle of expectation, sensory stimulation and action)" (2016: 176). The point of these rolling cycles, however, is for the experiencing agent to be action ready. Citing the work of Cisek and Kalaska (2010) on affordance competition, Clark suggests that "the neural representations involved are . . . 'pragmatic' insofar as 'they are adapted to produce good control [for a set of possible actions] as opposed to producing accurate descriptions of the sensory environment or a motor plan'" (Clark 2016: 180). The process is affordance-based and action-oriented. This idea, that our perception of the world is "constantly conditioned by our own 'action repertoire' . . . in interaction with our needs, projects, and opportunities" comes very close to the enactive view.

An alternative formulation of the third wave involves integrating enactive and extended approaches, pushing the analysis in a more dynamical direction (see Dale, Dietrich, & Chemero 2009; Menary 2010b; Kirchhoff 2012). Extended-mind and enactivist views agree that cognition is not constituted as the result of exclusively neurocentric processes in the head. They disagree, however, on two points typically defended by proponents of the EMH: the role of representation (including action-oriented representation [see Section 6.2]) and the functionalist downplaying of the importance of the specificities of the material body. Accordingly, despite some meeting of the minds, there is resistance on both sides, since enactive approaches reject functionalist and representationalist solutions as much as extended approaches embrace them. These same issues promise to derail any easy connections between a representationalist PP and enactive cognition. We will take up that challenge in Section 7.2.

For Clark, PP is consistent with "intermediate-level" functionalism (a computational level of processing between neural and behavioral levels) which grounds the extended mind (2016: 2). In his account one can still find a form of parity between the options of (a) revising predictions and models in order to reduce prediction errors in the brain's sensory input, and (b) taking action to manipulate the environment to accomplish the same trick. Actions "that engage and exploit specific external resources" get selected "in just the same manner as the inner coalitions of neural resources themselves" (2016: 260). Accordingly, the "upshot is a dynamic, self-organizing system to which the inner (and outer) flow of information is constantly reconfigured according to the demands of the task and the changing details of the internal (interoceptively sensed) and external context" (2016: 3).

If Hohwy's version of PP reflects all the hallmarks of CC – computational inference, mental representations, and a disembodied, neurocentric functionalism that discounts any essential role for the body, Clark dials back on these ideas. So, although on the one hand, Clark considers factors associated with anatomical determination and embodied semantics to be "trivial and uninteresting" rather than deeply "special" (2008b: 38), reflecting a functionalist perspective, on the other hand, he defends the notion that the body plays an important role as part of the extended mechanisms of cognition. As he puts it, "the larger systemic wholes, incorporating brains, bodies, the motion of sense organs, and (under some conditions) the information-bearing states of non-biological props and aids, may sometimes constitute the *mechanistic supervenience base* for mental states and processes" (2008b: 38).

How does extended cognition answer the challenge questions? I'll formulate some general responses without trying to differentiate the different theoretical waves.

1. *Which notion of embodiment is operative?* Extended cognition, like embedded cognition, emphasizes how a perceiving and agentive body couples with the environment. In contrast to embedded cognition, however, extended cognition claims a constitutive role for the body–environment, and various artifacts, props, technological instruments, with which we engage.

2. *Which sectors of cognition, or which cognitive tasks, are embodied; and how fully does each task involve embodiment?* Memory, belief, problem-solving, communicative practices, and epistemic actions more generally may depend on bodily interaction with the physical and social environment.

3. *What empirical evidence supports specific embodiment claims?* Research in experimental and ecological psychology, robotics, neuroscience, and cognitive archaeology supports a variety of claims made by extended cognition.

4. *How do the proffered claims depart substantially from CC?* Although extended cognition emphasizes the role of body–environment interactions that are not usually considered by CC, it also retains concepts of functionalism and representation that are not far removed from CC.

5. *What role do mental or neural representations play in cognition?* As we'll see in more detail in Section 6.2, extended cognition endorses action-oriented representations. Action-oriented representations are employed in navigating and negotiating the environment. They are action specific and context dependent, rather than heavy, semantic, content-laden representations that may be required for higher-order cognition, or what Clark and Toribio (1994) call "representation-hungry" processes.

We'll take up some of these issues again in the next section. For now, Table 1 provides a brief summary of the different interpretations of EC so far.

6 The Fourth E: Enactive Cognition

Enactive views on EC emphasize the idea that perception is *for action*, and that this action orientation shapes most cognitive processes. This approach calls for a radical change in the way we think about the mind and brain, with implications for how we do cognitive science. Varela, Thompson, and Rosch (1991), who first defined the enactive approach in their book *The Embodied Mind*, were inspired and informed by phenomenological philosophy, theoretical biology, and behavior-based robotics (Brooks 1991), as well as Buddhist philosophy and psychology. From phenomenology, enactive approaches draw on Husserl's pragmatic idea that I perceive things in terms of what *I can do* with them, which shapes our primary experience of the world as a prereflective, action-oriented operative intentionality (Merleau-Ponty 2012), rather than as a reflective intellectual contemplation or observation. These are ideas which led to Gibson's notion of affordances (as noted in Section 4), as well as to Hubert Dreyfus's critique of artificial intelligence.[4] In addition, in *The Embodied Mind* both

---

[4] Dreyfus is an important figure, not only for his early critique of AI but also for his influence on enactivism. Under the influence of Dreyfus (1982), Varela, Thompson, and Rosch (1991) favored the phenomenologies of Heidegger and Merleau-Ponty, and discounted the views of Husserl.

Table 1 Answers to the challenge questions

Interpretation	Weak EC	Embodied Semantics	Strong EC	Embedded	Extended
Sectors of cognition	Perception, higher-order, and social cognition	Higher-order cognition	Perception, action	Perception, learning, memory, problem-solving	Perception/action and higher-order cognition
Empirical evidence	Neuroscience (mirror neurons, lesions), behavioral studies	Linguistics, psychology, neuroscience, cultural anthropology	Biology, experimental psychology	Experimental and ecological psychology, evolutionary science, ethnographic studies	Experimental and ecological psychology, robotics, neuroscience, and cognitive archaeology
Consistent with CC	Yes	Yes, in part	Varies across researchers	Yes, in part	Yes
Representations	Yes, strongly representational, with B-formats playing special role	No	Varies across researchers	Varies across researchers	Yes for "representation-hungry" processes; action-oriented representations for perception/action

phenomenology and Buddhist practices were thought to offer methodological insight to first-person experience which, for enactive cognitive science, is integrated with third-person scientific data, in what Francisco Varela (1996) called neurophenomenology.

Varela, working with Humberto Maturana in the 1970s, formulated a biological theory of autopoiesis which strongly informs the enactive approach. Autopoiesis explains how a living system autonomously organizes and sustains itself in a process of self-production. Maturana and Varela (1980/1972: 78) describe it as involving a pattern of processes which:

(i) through their interactions and transformations continuously regenerate and realize the network of processes (relations) that produced them; and
(ii) constitute [the living system] as a concrete unity in space in which they (the components) exist by specifying the topological domain of its realization as such a network.

In other words, the organism produces the components which continue to sustain the organized structure that gives rise to these components, and in that process defines its own bounded identity. Varela refers to this as operational closure.[5] Operational closure means that the system "generates and specifies its own organization through its operation as a system of production of its own components" (1980/1972: 79). This does not mean that the organism is causally closed to the environment, however. Rather, it is structurally coupled to the environment, drawing energy from it, and adapting to changing circumstances (Di Paolo 2005). Adaptivity involves the organism, which is never in perfect equilibrium, engaging in a precarious process of regulating itself with respect to maintaining stable, dynamic viability. This kind of differential engagement with the environment is considered a form of basic cognition – a form of sense-making capable of registering environmental differences. Autopoietic enactivism thus argues for a strong continuity between life and mind. The organizational features of life are the same as the organizational features of mind; mind, in this sense, is a particular form of life (Thompson 2007).

Basic cognition, accordingly, is defined as an organism's response to, or its way of adaptively coupling to the environment. Cognition, in this case, is fully embodied, and depends on the specific kind of body involved to specify structures and properties in the environment that bear on the organism's existence.

They later came to regard Husserl's work on the notion of the lived body and temporality as important for enactive philosophy (see e.g., Varela 1999; Thompson 2007).

[5] Varela used the term "organizational closure" when writing with Maturana and in his early papers; he shifts to "operational closure" in his later work. Evan Thompson suggests that operational closure is more dynamic (2007: 45).

Accordingly, in the case of human bodies with complex evolved brains and nervous systems, cognition will be different from cognition in nonhuman animals. An organism "meets the environment on its own sensorimotor terms," and brings forth what counts as meaningful (Thompson 2005: 418); in this sense it enacts its world. It specifies its *Umwelt* or lifeworld as relative to its own form of organization.

> In a nutshell, the enactive approach consists of two points: (1) perception consists in perceptually guided action and (2) cognitive structures emerge from the recurrent sensorimotor patterns that allow action to be perceptually guided. (Varela et al. 1991: 173)

Thompson and Varela (2001) endorse an additional three points in summary of the enactive view, based on Clark (1999).

(3) Understanding the complex interplay of brain, body, and world requires the tools and methods of nonlinear dynamical systems theory;

(4) traditional notions of representation and computation are inadequate;

(5) traditional decompositions of the cognitive system into inner functional sub-systems or modules ("boxology") are misleading, and blind us to arguably better decompositions into dynamical systems that cut across the brain–body–world divisions. (Thompson & Varela 2001: 418; also see Chemero 2009: 29)

For enactivism, then, cognitive processes do not replicate a perceiver- or agent-independent world by means of a representational mapping or internal model; rather, cognition is characterized by affordance-related engagements. In contrast to classic cognitive science, which is often characterized by methodo-logical individualism and a focus on internal mechanisms, enactive approaches emphasize the relational and socially situated nature of human cognitive sys-tems. Enactive approaches also aim to ground higher and more complex cogni-tive functions not only in sensorimotor coordination, but also in affective and autonomic aspects of the full body; higher-order cognitive functions, such as reflective thinking and deliberation, are exercises of skillful know-how and are usually coupled with situated and embodied actions.

In the following sections we'll discuss each of these principles and along the way show how enactive views incorporate many of the aspects of embodied, embedded, and extended approaches, but also reject any tenets that would keep some of these approaches too close to classic cognitivism.

6.1 Dynamical Integration

Similar to the idea of extended cognition, enactive approaches argue that cognition is not entirely "in the head," but distributed across an integrated system of brain, body, and world, where world involves both physical and social environments. In contrast to Clark's functionalist view, however, enactive theorists claim that (human) bodily processes shape and contribute to the constitution of consciousness and cognition in an irreducible and irreplaceable way. Enactive accounts emphasize bodily capacities, including most of the processes emphasized by strong EC (Section 3.3) rather than committing to more abstract computational or information-processing accounts (Hutto 2005). Specifically, on the enactive view, biological aspects of bodily life, including organismic and emotion regulation, have a permeating effect on cognition (Colombetti 2014; Thompson 2007), as do processes of sensorimotor coupling between organism and environment.

Different versions of enactivism have been motivated by different emphases in enactive theorists, typically with lines drawn between autopoietic enactivism, sensorimotor enactivism, and radical enactivism (e.g., Ward, Silverman, & Villalobos 2017). Indeed, within enactive approaches, as in EC more generally, or any other philosophically informed research program, one can find disagreements in every corner. Although such distinctions can clearly be made, the landscape of enactive approaches seems to me to be more complex, marked with developments, extensions, and various degrees of integration, all of which may signal the growing pains of a novel research program. Many of the differences and disagreements, I'll argue, are the result of addressing different sets of issues – in some cases, ontological; in others, methodological; and in still others phenomenological. In the following sections, then, I'll note significant differences, but I won't try to systematize them.

Consider sensorimotor enactivists like Alva Noë (2004; also, Hurley 1998; O'Regan & Noë 2001) who, drawing on some of the same sources as Varela et al., including Merleau-Ponty (2012) and Gibson (1979), developed a detailed account of enactive perception where sensory-motor contingencies and environmental affordances take over some of the work that classic cognitivism had attributed to neural computations and mental representations. Sensorimotor enactive accounts of perception stress patterns of body–environment interaction and active motoric engagement in place of internal representations. Perception is constituted by the exercise of sensorimotor capacities, and in this regard, is a kind of skillful action. Studies by Hafed and Krauzlis (2006), for example, show that eye movement can help to disambiguate sensory input, enabling perceivers to resolve ambiguity in the retinal signal. For any possible bodily movement, sensory patterns change in lawlike ways, and the agent's grasp of such contingencies is an essential part of what constitutes perception. On this view, then, what the perceiver perceives is a function of relations that hold between patterns of sensory processes and motor processes, and the perceiver's attunement to the environment depends on an implicit attunement to these sensorimotor dependencies.

Consider a common example of sensorimotor contingency. If I turn my head, the object in front of me changes its location in my visual field. As Gangopadhyay and Kiverstein (2009) note, these processes of active perception depend on dynamical feedback in which sensory and motor processes are in a reciprocal relation – dynamic perception-action-perception cycles that couple the perceiver with the environment. The perceiver is implicitly attuned to this kind of systematic contingency. Being attuned to it simply means that I, as a perceiver, anticipate this will happen; I "keep track" of it (Hurley 1998: 140). The agentive system's ability to keep track of such sensory consequences allows it to distinguish its own self-generated movements from movements that are not self-generated – an ability to distinguish self and nonself, and part of what forms a perspectival self-awareness. Having a perspective in this sense is tied to agency.

> At the personal level, having a perspective means that what you experience and perceive depends systematically on what you do, as well as vice versa. Moreover, it involves your keeping track, even if not in conceptual terms, of the interdependence between what is perceived and what is done, and hence awareness of your own agency. (Hurley 1998: 86)

These processes of keeping track are not necessarily conscious, although they can become conscious, and, as Alva Noë (2004) suggests, may even involve a conceptual knowledge that is not just knowledge about what I see, and a sense of self, but also knowledge about the world that I experience. This would suggest a dynamical integration between perception, action, and conceptual-inferential skills.[6] One can see this kind of integration, for example, in how one's conscious intention can determine very basic, nonconscious, visual-motoric saccadic processes. Mark Rowlands (2006) cites Alfred Yarbus's (1967) experiments on saccadic eye movements. Yarbus asked subjects to answer different questions about a painting they were viewing. For example, judge the age of the people in the painting, guess what the people had been doing prior to the arrival of the visitor, or remember the clothing worn by the people depicted in the painting. Each task elicited a different visual saccadic scan pattern. Likewise, Gangopadhyay and Kiverstein (2009: 71) cite numerous empirical studies demonstrating that "it is the task the agent is performing that determines where the agent directs her gaze, not the properties of a scene."

> Saccades are an action system in that they are a visually controlled motor response. However they are not just this, since their operation controls the

---

[6] This could be read as a difference from an earlier subpersonal nonconceptual view, as in O'Regan & Noë (2001), but it can also be understood as simply a different emphasis that addresses "different explanatory purposes" (Ward et al. 2017).

input visual sampling also. Their involvement with vision takes the form of
a continuously cycling loop, so that vision and cognition can integrate in an
intimate way. (Findlay & Gilchrist 2003: 7)

In other words, such basic eye movements are one way in which a perceiver
dynamically couples to the environment, and this coupling is shaped by the task
or intention of the perceiver.

In addition to sensorimotor contingencies, enactive theorists emphasize the
role of affectivity. Giovanna Colombetti, whose work is highly influenced by
autopoietic enactivism, argues for an intrinsic link between affectivity, generally conceived, and cognition. She takes emotions, for example, to be dynamical
patterns, "self-organizing patterns of the organism, best described with the
conceptual tools of dynamical systems theory (DST)," involving "multiple
simultaneous interactions" of brain, body, and world (2014: 53). Emotional
patterns are "context dependent, flexible, and 'loosely assembled' and yet can
also display stability across contexts" (57). Broadly conceived, affectivity
involves autopoietic processes connected with metabolism, homeostatic, (or
homeodynamic) processes (Colombetti 2014: xv).

The importance of affectivity is not always considered by proponents of
sensory-motor contingency (see Bower & Gallagher 2013 for this criticism).
Although affective processes are not reducible to sensorimotor processes,
clearly they are dynamically integrated with such processes. For example,
depressed affect may slow down motor-control processes (Caligiuri &
Ellwanger 2000). Degenaar and O'Regan (2017), however, suggest that sensorimotor responses to the environment already include affective factors.
According to them, one doesn't have to look beyond sensorimotor processes
themselves to explain this. It's not clear, however, that even if an emotion
pattern *in part* includes sensorimotor processes or action tendencies, other,
nonsensorimotor aspects of emotion, for example, autonomic or evaluative
aspects, do not impact perception. Affectivity, taken in the broadest sense to
include factors such as energy level, fatigue, hunger, pain, emotion, mood, and
so on, impinges on our sensorimotor capabilities (as demonstrated, for example,
by Proffitt's experiments discussed in Sections 3.1 and 3.3). I perceive the
object in front of me as something I can reach and grab, but affectivity may
determine whether I have the interest or inclination or energy to do so, in which
case such affective factors can modulate the sensorimotor processes that figure
into my action, slowing them down, for example. Pain or fear may even cause
my typical sensorimotor abilities to dissipate. The idea that affective and
sensorimotor factors are tightly and dynamically integrated components of
embodied processes is also shown by Fogel and Thelen (1987). On their

analysis, emotion patterns emerge from the mutual influences of various bodily and environmental processes across different timescales. These include neural, respiratory, and musculature dynamics that can mutually influence each other.

6.2 Doing without Representations

A representation, in cognitive science, is most generally conceived as something that stands in for something else, as a surrogate within a computational process, explaining why the process is about a particular object or event. Standard or traditional conceptions claim that a mental or neural representation has specific properties, for example, that it bears content that references something other than itself, that it can be decoupled from a particular context so that it can represent something that is absent, that it has satisfaction (or truth) conditions, and that it can interact with other representations. It is often thought that EC approaches, even if they differ among themselves, are united in their opposition to traditional versions of representationalism. As we have seen in the previous sections, however, this is clearly not the case. Indeed, disagreements within the EC camp are primarily disagreements about just these issues. Perhaps one important outcome of the EC debates is that they have moved the issues about computationalism and representationalism front and center, even in the minds of those who have taken less-embodied approaches. Thus, there have been wholesale investigations into the concept of representation (e.g., Ramsey 2007; Smortchkova, Dolega, & Schlicht 2020), as well as careful and somewhat defensive explanations of what representation means in analytic philosophy of mind (e.g., Burge 2010; Crane 2008). On all sides, however, the conceptual landscape is littered with promissory notes. Specifically in regard to EC, Anthony Chemero (2009) makes it clear that it will be important to "scale up" dynamic systems approaches from the analysis of action and perception to higher cognitive performance in what are considered to be "representation-hungry" tasks (Clark & Toribio 1994). "It is still an open-question how far beyond minimally cognitive behaviors radical embodied cognitive science can get" (Chemero 2009: 43). This seems especially relevant to enactive accounts which attempt to banish representations as much as possible (Gallagher 2017; Hutto & Myin 2013). So far, Chemero suggests, on this score, we have only a promissory note.

The first problem is that more than one concept of representation operates in cognitive science. Besides the divide (if there is a divide) between mental and neural representations, the concept ranges from fully semantic, truth-conditional, propositional structures that serve to specify the way the world is (Fodor 2008), to minimal action-oriented representations that serve motor control (Clark 1997; Millikan 1995), to a variety of deflated concepts, including (1) the idea that representation is a simple co-variance between internal processes and environmental stimuli, (2) the idea that representations are fictional but useful tools for scientific explanation, or (3) the idea of content-free mechanistic representations. A second problem is that, despite various attempts, there is no agreed-upon explanation of how representational mechanisms (or vehicles) actually come to have content – that is, how they capture and carry meaningful information about things in the world. Hutto and Myin, defending a radical enactive view of cognition (REC), call this the "hard problem of content," and as they put it, cognitive science needs to provide "accounts of the origin of mental content; how mental contents could be carried by vehicles; and how mental contents might matter" (2020: 83; see also Akins 1996 for a detailed discussion of related problems). To the extent that such accounts are lacking, these questions indicate some important promissory notes on the representationalist side.

Although it will not be possible to review all of the arguments for or against representations in this section (for such arguments see Ramsey 2007; Smortchkova, Dolega, & Schlicht 2020), we will discuss (1) why even minimal or deflated concepts of representation are unacceptable to enactive approaches; and (2) what a nonrepresentationalist enactive explanation looks like.

We have already discussed the idea of body- or B-formatted representations in Section 3.1. Here we'll start with the concept of action-oriented representation (AOR), proposed as part of the EMH. We noted (in Section 5.3) that AORs are employed in navigating and negotiating the environment. They are action specific and context dependent. They are not the semantically heavy, content-laden representations that, according to CC, may be required for higher-order cognition, or "representation-hungry" processes. Michael Wheeler (2005), following Clark (1997: 47ff., 149ff.), suggests that AORs are temporary egocentric motor maps of the environment, fully determined by the situation-specific action required. Action-oriented representations do not represent the objectively pre-existing world, or map it out in a neuronal pattern. Rather, they encode the world in terms of the agent's possibilities for action (Wheeler 2005: 197); their action-specific representational function enables controlled situated actions. This sounds like an enactive representation, if there ever were such a thing.

Clark and Grush (1999) offer a model of anticipatory motor-control processes that involve AORs instantiated in the "internal" neural circuitry of a forward model or emulator, that is, a mechanism that predicts sensory feedback resulting from an action. The circuitry forms a "decouplable surrogate," that is, a representation that stands in for a future state of some extraneural aspect of a particular movement; the representation of either an impending just-about-to-be-accomplished body position, or the expected proprioceptive feedback connected with such movement. For example, the AOR may represent the trajectory of an outfielder's reach as she prepares to catch a ball that is coming toward her. Since the emulator represents or stands in for some motor state that is not yet actualized, it is in some sense offline or decoupled from the current state of movement. Clark and Grush explain that this AOR, which they call a "minimal robust representation" is an inner state that does not depend "on a constant physical linkage" between it and the extraneural bodily states which it is about. Thus, "emulators seem to be a nice, biologically detailed example of the sort of disengagement that Brian Cantwell Smith (1996) . . . argued to be crucial for understanding representation" (Clark & Grush 1999: 7). Smith, however, thinks it's very difficult to conceive of egocentric representations as disengaged or context independent since they are "closely related to our sense of self, to our personal identity" (Smith 1996: 248).

I'll return to the point about how they relate to self. Concerning context independence, however, Smith suggests that representations can be considered context independent only as a matter of degree: "the idea of a completely context-independent or 'non-deictic' representation is a fiction" (1996: 248). Indeed, it is difficult to see how an aspect of motor control, a constitutive part of the action, can be considered decoupled from the moving body it is tracking, or, for that matter, from the action and action context. Isn't the kind of anticipatory process Clark and Grush describe fully situated in the action context? In the case of catching a ball, for example, anticipations of where the ball will be in the next second, and where my hand needs to be to catch it, require reference to the present state of the system, including the current motor command (or efference copy in the forward model) – informed and updated by ongoing perception and proprioceptive feedback about the current location of the ball and of my hand, respectively. Just as we can perceive the ball's trajectory, so we can feel in kinesthetic terms the temporal and spatial trajectory of our action. In what sense do such processes involve a disengagement or decoupling, rather than a dynamical physical linkage – relying on the physical processes of my eyes tracking the ball, activating extraocular muscles and kinesthetic sense, and my hand already in movement, generating its own proprioceptive/kinesthetic feedback? Clark and Grush seem to allow for this interpretation: "The case of basic motor emulation does indeed fall short of meeting this stricter criterion [of decoupleability] . . . the surrogate states are not fully decoupleable from ongoing environmental input." Instead, they instantiate "a kind of fine tuning for environmentally coupled action" (1999: 10).

To the extent that AORs do not fit standard definitions of representations, which include the idea that they can be decoupled, why not take a nonrepresentationalist view in regard to the sort of example that Clark and Grush discuss? In fact, Clark (2008b) moves closer to an ecological-enactive, nonrepresentational account that involves a direct sensing.

> Sensing here acts as a constantly available channel that productively couples agent and environment rather than as a kind of "veil of transduction" whereby world-originating signals must be converted into a persisting inner model of the external scene . . . . [T]he point is simply that the canny use of data available in the optic flow enables the catcher to sidestep the need to create a rich inner model to calculate the forward trajectory of the ball. In such cases, as Randall Beer puts it, "the focus shifts from accurately representing an environment to continuously engaging that environment with a body so as to stabilize appropriate co-ordinated patterns of behavior" (2000: 97). (Clark 2008a: 15–16)

The often-referenced outfielder who successfully catches the ball does so, not by representing or computing the ball's trajectory, but by running to keep the position of the ball stationary in her line of sight (Clark 2015; Fink, Foo, & Warren 2009). The alternative enactive account rejects AORs in favor of action-oriented bodily engagements describable in dynamical terms.

In their enactivist critique of the concept of representation, Hutto and Myin (2020) focus on the notion of representational content. They repeat an often-repeated complaint that standard representational concepts of mind have never adequately explained how representational vehicles actually carry content, that is, how they have meaningful reference or intentionality (Clapin 2002; Smith 1996). This is the hard problem of content again (Hutto & Satne 2015). Deflationary accounts of representation may count as offering an alternative that escapes this hard problem. Deflationary claims tend to move away from or downplay any strong claims about content. Representations may consist of just the mechanistic (vehicle) processes, which is all one needs for explanatory purposes (Chomsky1995); or they may just be scientific fictions that pragmatically facilitate our explanations, but have no ontological existence.

Consider, for example, Frances Egan's (2014) deflationary view which, with some nuance, banishes semantic (or cognitive) content but posits a mathematical content. We can think of mathematical content as the algorithm, or computational (purely syntactical) function that a system follows in processing information related to a specific task. Egan claims that the computational process introduces mathematical content instantiated in neural representational vehicles. What we typically think of as cognitive or semantic content is what we attribute to the representation in light of the role it plays in a particular cognitive task. According to Egan, however, this cognitive content is nothing more than an "intentional gloss" – an interpretation made by an observer of the system. It may be helpful for developing an explanation, but the mathematical content, rather than the cognitive content, does the actual work.

> Cognitive contents ... are not part of the essential characterization of the device, and are not fruitfully regarded as part of the computational theory proper. They are ascribed to facilitate the explanation of the cognitive capacity in question and are sensitive to a host of pragmatic considerations. (Egan 2014: 128).

In contrast to Ramsey (2020), who counts both types of content (mathematical and cognitive) as essential, and who wants to push Egan toward a realist position on cognitive content, Hutto and Myin (2020) push the other way. They note that, according to Egan, mathematical content is essential (or intrinsic), context neutral, and abstract. As such, it serves a "variety of different cognitive uses in different contexts" (Egan 2014: 122).[7] Egan's account avoids what is typically considered a problem – the intensional indeterminacy of cognitive content (the idea that it's difficult to say whether a particular neural state represents some object, some time-slice of the object, some property of the object, or some related event). For Egan, this is a pragmatic or hermeneutical problem of simply getting the intentional gloss right. What really counts is the mathematical characterization. Hutto and Myin relate this to a PP model. They cite Clark's characterization of generative models, which at some level capture not how the world is in a way that matters to the agent, but simply "precision-weight estimates ... that drive action," in ways that are not understandable "using the vocabulary of the ordinary daily speech" (Clark 2016: 292; cited in Hutto & Myin 2020: 93). Likewise, Karl Friston, who in some cases seems to support a narrow internalist version of PP (e.g., Hohwy, Roepstorff, & Friston 2008), and in other cases, a more extended version (Constant, Clark, & Friston 2021), and in even other cases an enactive version of PP (Allen & Friston 2018), has indicated that for him the important issue concerns, not the philosophical interpretations, but getting the mathematical models right (private communication). Thus, in the most basic sense, in these PP contexts it's the mathematical content that is important.

---

[7] One argument is that the mathematical content is essential to the representational process because it can remain the same from one context to another while the cognitive content would change with each context. On this view, a representation is *essentially* syntactical; how it connects to meaning or semantics depends on an external and variable interpretation. Bechtel and Huang (2022: 61) point out that this argument is of the same type as Searle's Chinese Room argument in the context of AI.

Hutto and Myin suggest two problems that still haunt such deflated accounts. First, as Egan admits, "it is not likely that mathematical content could be naturalized" (2014: 123), since it is instantiated in purely formal operations that are independent of any external or internal environment and neutral with respect to any material process. This, according to Hutto and Myin, is just the hard problem of content once again. Second, such accounts lead Egan and Clark to think of mathematical content as having causal power – the mathematical content is doing some work. "Yet, to this day it is unclear how contents qua contents ... can influence the behavior of states of a system so as to causally explain what the system does" (Hutto & Myin 2020: 95). This is Jaegwon Kim's causal exclusion problem: Simply put, if the neuronal mechanisms are doing the causal work, awarding causal power to content of any sort would be redundant. If, then, we assume that the mathematical contents are not playing a causal role, it's not clear what explanatory gain they provide beyond another heuristic gloss, and in that case they would not be essential to cognition.

To clarify this argument, consider Smith's example of a robot designed to pick up Coke cans. He considers that this may involve an internal memory representation, but one that could be interpreted as an AOR, since it is guiding the robot's action. If the robot sees a Coke can x feet in front of it and y feet to the right, it registers $\langle x,y \rangle$. It then moves toward the can until it reaches $\langle o, o \rangle$. It then scoops up the can. The question, as Smith specifies, is what precisely the representational content is, and he provides some alternatives.

(1) It egocentrically represents a *particular place*: that stable point on the floor x feet in front and y feet to the right of the robot's current position.

(2) It egocentrically represents *the Coke can* lying at that position. The memory register is only used when there is a Coke can there, after all, and it is Coke cans, not positions, toward which the overall behavior of the system is directed.

(3) Rather than egocentrically representing the position of either a place or a can, it allocentrically represents the position of the robot with reference to the position of the Coke can ....

(4) Rather than having any particular content, in terms of specific individuals or places, it instead represents the generic property of being x feet in front and y to the right.

(5) It is not a representation at all, and so has no content. Rather, it is a simple control state in a digital servo mechanism. (Smith 1996: 51)

As Smith suggests, without more information we can't say which of these interpretations is correct. Adopting any one of them seems arbitrary. We can think, however, that (4) picks out the mathematical content. As stated, however, it is incomplete. One would need to say not just that it "represents the generic property of being x feet in front and y to the right," *period*, but more specifically, "x feet in front and y to the right *of the robot*." Perhaps this is already implicit in the egocentric terms of (4). Smith speaks of the representation as being pragmatically actionable, "in the sense of being more easily converted into motor signals" (1996: 248). Without reference to what we might call self-location (even if, in the robotic example, this is not a sense of self or personal identity), (4) would not be very useful. In that case, the particularity involved in (1) would be a more appropriate interpretation; this would be a minimal basis for saying that such a representation is narcissistic, as Kathleen Akins (1996) puts it, in the sense that its purpose is not to represent the world, but rather to represent how the world is relevant to the agent's action. Moreover, we may prefer (2) if the robot is going to do the work we want it to do. One could argue here that, *pace* Hutto and Myin, even if the robotic mechanisms are doing the causal work, the mathematical content is surely assisting, guiding the robot to the Coke can. With (2), however, we are back to the Clark–Grush conception of AOR, and we can ask again, going with something like option (5), why we should consider this a representation at all, rather than an action-oriented physical engagement describable in dynamical terms, as one finds in Rodney Brook's robots that use the world rather than an internal representation to navigate. Indeed, Clark and Grush admit that "the emulator circuitry can also and simultaneously be viewed simply as a smaller dynamical system linked to the one that hooks directly into the real-world" (1999: 8). In this respect, however, they opt to address a pragmatic question: "The question is, which of these descriptions is most useful for Cognitive Science?" Their answer loops back to Egan's idea, and Hutto and Myin's objection, that talk of representation here is, as Clark and Grush themselves say, "a representational gloss" (Clark & Grush 1999: 8). They nonetheless want to hold that the forward (emulator) processes in motor control involve something real and that the representational gloss captures it. Even if the robot goes straight for the Coke can, we seem to be going in (theoretical) circles.

If we are to move beyond this impasse in what Constant, Clark, and Friston (2021) have characterized as the "representation wars," it is important to say what enactivism offers as the alternative to representational explanations. When one looks for this alternative, one finds a different vocabulary – not "representation," "content," "information processing," or "computational coding," but rather "attunement," "embodied engagement," "dynamical coupling," "sensory-motor contingencies," and "affordance." Behind this shift in vocabulary there is, importantly, a shift in assumptions, including assumptions about what constitutes an explanation. If we start by framing the problem in internalist terms that characterize the brain as the exclusive seat of cognition, or in strict functionalist terms where, on the principle of multiple realizability, any physical state or process capable of implementing or realizing the relevant functional requirements will do, then a representationalist account may seem to be the only game in town. In contrast, if we characterize the problem in a way that takes the brain–body–environment as the explanatory unit, and if we maintain that the biological and extended nature of the system makes a significant difference, then an account in terms of attunements and affordances seems more relevant. There are other issues about whether the explanation should be mechanistic-causal, or whether the kinds of equations derived in dynamical systems theory count as explanations (Chemero 2001). At some point one might be tempted to think that we should simply look at the empirical evidence to decide the issue. In the previous section we cited a good amount of experimental evidence that would seem to support many of the claims made by EC and by enactive accounts. The problem with this strategy is that both sides can cite the very same data but offer different interpretations. In this regard, it's not that either the representationalist or the nonrepresentationalist account is nonscientific (for discussions about the legitimate use of the concept of representation and its utility in cognitive science, see Ramsey 2007, and Shea 2018). It's rather a matter of the question posed by Clark and Grush: "which of these descriptions is most useful for Cognitive Science?" (Clark & Grush 1999: 8).

These issues – what terms to use, what's useful, what counts as scientific explanation, and so forth – remain open questions that are driving current debates. One example, to which we will return in Section 7, is whether PP can operate as a common ground to sort out these issues. We've already seen that PP accounts shift across internalist and extended versions, and that the assumptions made by the embodied-extended mind version (involving functionalism and representationalism) are not going to match up with enactive approaches. The emphasis placed on active inference by Clark, however, may set the stage for an enactive PP account. The notion of active inference underscores the importance of embodiment and dynamical interaction (Friston, Mattout, & Kilner 2011; Kilner, Friston, & Frith 2007). On the enactive model, active inference is not so much inference as ongoing predictive engagement – a set of dynamical adjustments in which the brain, as part of and along with the larger organism, actively responds in ways that allow for the right kind of ongoing attunement with the environment – an environment that is physical but also social and cultural. Processes of dynamical adjustment/attune-ment encompass the whole of the system and are not a mere testing or sampling that serves better neural prediction (cf. Clark 2016: 7; Hohwy 2013: 79). Rather, active engagement is an attuned doing, a worldly engagement – with anticipatory and corrective aspects already included. This would be one way to cash out Merleau-Ponty's claim: "My body has its world, or understands its world without having to go through 'representations,' or without being subordinated to a 'symbolic' or 'objectifying function'" (2012: 141).

Enactive approaches argue that the brain is not the operative center of the system, conducting tests that sample the external world; it's rather one station or one complex set of circuits among other stations within a system that includes body and environment and forms the whole. Neural accommodation occurs via constant reciprocal interaction between the brain and body, and notions of adjustment and attunement can be cashed out in terms of physical dynamical processes that include autonomic and peripheral nervous systems (Gallagher et al. 2013; Gallagher & Allen 2018). Whether an integration of PP and enactive theory can work as part of an alternative to representationalist accounts will depend on some further theoretical and technical considerations. We return to this point in Section 7.2. First, however, we want to fulfill some of the promissory notes that continue to appear in some enactive accounts.

6.3 Intersubjectivity

From the enactive perspective, considerations about intersubjective interaction are not secondary or peripheral problems relevant just to social cognition and how we understand others. Rather, issues pertaining to social cognition in a wide sense, including how we engage with others in intersubjective sense-making, are regarded as intrinsically relevant to understanding perception, memory, action, problem-solving, and so forth. Furthermore, in contrast to standard, overly cognitive approaches (where understanding others is construed as "mindreading," based on theoretical inference or simulation, typically called theory of mind [ToM]), enactivists take intersubjective interactions to be fully embodied perceptual and motoric processes, involving facial expression, posture, movement, gestures, vocal intonations, and specific forms of sensory-motor couplings in highly contextualized pragmatic and social environments.

Enactivists appeal to developmental studies that show that from early infancy, humans engage in embodied intersubjective practices, a phenomenon Colwyn Trevarthen (1979) calls "primary intersubjectivity." Infants engage with caregivers in mutual, second-person, back-and-forth responses involving bodily movements and expressions that reflect affectivity and action intention, a form of "intercorporeity" (Merleau-Ponty 2012), which depends on perceiving the other person in a way that resonates kinetically and kinesthetically (Meltzoff et al. 2018). As early as at two months, infants are already attuned to the other person's attention; they follow the other's head movements and gaze

(Baron-Cohen 1997). They "vocalize and gesture in a way that seems [affectively and temporally] 'tuned' to the vocalizations and gestures of the other person" (Gopnik & Meltzoff 1997: 131). This interactive attunement involves a mutual alignment that can be specified in detail in dynamical coordination studies (Alviar, Kello, & Dale 2023; De Jaegher & Di Paolo 2007; Goodwin 2000; Murray & Trevarthen 1985; Zhang et al. 2020). Mirror-neuron activations may be part of such processes. In this context, such activations are understood as part of the neural processes involved in the perception of the other's motor intentions, instantiating anticipatory response preparation to perceived action, rather than a simulation or simple mirroring of mental states (Gallagher 2020). Importantly, the interactions that compose primary intersubjectivity are not automatic procedures; Csibra and Gergely (2009) have shown that the infant is more likely to respond to another person's actions only if that person is attending to the infant.

Context and social environment also contribute to "secondary intersubjective" practices starting at nine to twelve months of age (Trevarthen & Hubley 1978). This is when infants are able to engage in joint attention and joint actions, and they begin to grasp the meaning of the other person's actions in rich pragmatic and social contexts.

> The defining feature of secondary intersubjectivity is that an object or event can become a focus between people. Objects and events can be communicated about . . . . [T]he infant's interactions with another person begin to have reference to the things that surround them. (Hobson 2002: 62)

If enactive perception is understood to be primarily "for action," then in the intersubjective context, perception is often for *inter*action with others, where perceptually guided interaction becomes a principle of social cognition and generates meaning in a process of "participatory sense-making" (De Jaegher & Di Paolo 2007; De Jaegher, Di Paolo, & Gallagher 2010).

To see the difference between a cognitivist approach and the enactive one, consider the standard false-belief experiments. Proponents of "theory theory," who construe social cognition to be a form of folk-psychological inference, often appeal to these experiments as evidence of a significant developmental change in social cognition. Standard false-belief tests have been administered to young children aged three to five years. One typical paradigm is to introduce a story, or a portrayal using toy figures or puppets; for example, a person, call him Maxi, hides a toy in a box, and then leaves the room (Wimmer & Perner 1983). A second person, call her Mini, moves the toy from the box to a basket, unbeknownst to Maxi. When Maxi returns, the child is asked by the experimenter where Maxi will look for the toy. On average, three-year-olds will say that Maxi will look in the basket, where the toy is now located; four-year-olds will say that Maxi will look in the box where Maxi left the toy, since Maxi does not know that Mini moved the toy. That is, the four-year-old will recognize that Maxi has a false belief about where the toy is. This recognition is said to be a form of mind reading based on a folk-psychological inference about Maxi's mental state, that is, about a belief that Maxi has. This test suggests that three-year-olds, and most children with autism, have not yet gained a ToM and are unable to understand that someone could have a false belief or a belief different from their own belief about where the toy is (Baron-Cohen 1997). Evidence from such standard false-belief tests led some theorists to conclude that at around four years of age, on average, a theory-of-mind module in the child's brain reaches a developmental stage to allow such mind reading (Saxe & Kanwisher 2003).

On the enactivist view, the standard false-belief test is at best a test for a specialized practice of third-person understanding that involves taking an observational standpoint on another's behavior. That is, the child is not interacting with Maxi, but is asked, somewhat abstractly, to say what Maxi might be thinking or how Maxi will behave. It shows that the four-year-old, on average, is able to deal with this challenge, but that the three-year-old is not. Despite the three-year-old's difficulty in identifying Maxi's mental state from a third-person perspective, children of this age typically have no problem understanding the experimenter with whom they are interacting. They pick up on all kinds of cues in their engagement with the experimenter – not only vocal communications, but such things as head nods to direct attention, vocal intonation that signals a question, turn-taking pauses that signal that it's the child's turn to speak, and so on. This is an embodied engagement with the experimenter that three-year-old children are quite capable of. They seem to understand what the experimenter intends, or at least what he or she expects of them. Perhaps they also understand that the experimenter is being very nice, cooperative, or friendly, in contrast to others who might be simply indifferent. The enactivist is suggesting here that bodily interaction is playing an important role in such second-person instances of social cognition, in a way that is not at all tested by the false-belief paradigm, but that nonetheless shows up in the experimental situation.

More recently, evidence from spontaneous-response false-belief tasks shows that infants as young as thirteen months manifest sensitivity to another's (false) beliefs; these tests use behavioral measures (e.g., anticipatory and preferential gazing, fixation time) rather than the direct questioning used in the standard test (Baillargeon, Scott, & Bian 2016; Onishi & Baillargeon 2005). Is the infants' success due to their ToM module maturing earlier than standardly thought (Carruthers 2013)? Or is it because in these tests real people, rather than toy figures or puppets, are used, and infants have been interacting with real people throughout the first year of life? Although these experiments keep the infant in an observational stance (rather than allowing interaction), the enactivist could still appeal to a violation of affordance expectation. That is, the infant's grasp of the other's behavior will depend on the infant's perception of social affordances (possibilities for interaction) even if the infant is not in a position to act on them. The more parsimonious explanation will appeal to processes that are closer to perception and interaction, than to metarepresentational and mentalizing abilities. Indeed, if you adjust some details of the standard false-belief paradigm to allow for interaction between the child and Maxi, the three-year-old does much better in providing the right answer (Rubio-Fernández & Geurts 2013). In one test, where eighteen-month-old infants are able to interact with and assist a real person looking for the toy, they pass the test with flying colors (Buttelmann, Carpenter, & Tomasello 2009).

One might still ask, however, why the four-year-old is able to do better in the third-person test? Perhaps, as the standard ToM theorist would have it, at four years old we shift from second-person interactive strategies to mind reading when our ToM module is activated. Enactivists disagree. They argue that primary and secondary intersubjectivity are not stages that we leave behind as we mature, but that interaction remains the primary way that we engage with others. That doesn't mean that we don't develop more subtle and sophisticated strategies for understanding others. Besides the direct interaction of primary intersubjectivity, and the pragmatic contextualized interaction involved in secondary intersubjectivity, at around three to four years of age children gain communicative and narrative competencies that allow them to more easily take third-person perspectives on others (Gallagher & Hutto 2008). Competency with different kinds of narratives enables us to understand others in a variety of ways. As Daniel Hutto suggests, "children normally achieve [folk-psychological] understanding by engaging in storytelling practices, with the support of others. The stories about those who act for reasons – i.e., folk psychological narratives – are the foci of this practice. Stories of this special kind provide the crucial training set needed for understanding reasons" (Hutto 2007: 53). This is what Hutto calls the "narrative practice hypothesis."

Evidence supporting this hypothesis can be found in developmental studies that show important links between narrative abilities and our capacity to understand others (Astington 1990; Dunn 1991; Feldman et al. 1990; Nelson 2007). For example, in storytelling practices, children are actively supported, perhaps by prompts to answer certain questions, and/or by directing their attention to certain features of a story, which may include the vocabulary of folk psychology, that the story character "knows," "feels," or "wants" something, and so on. Children learn from stories, as well as from everyday narratives within a household or school or play setting, how such concepts behave in relation to each other. Indeed, when children listen to stories, or engage in play-acting, they become familiarized with what actions are appropriate in specific situations. This helps to shape their expectations about how people will act, what actions are acceptable and in what circumstances, and what sorts of events are significant. Narratives provide a wide context for such understanding, so that children learn how and why these attitudes matter. Reasons for acting in a particular way are put on show, and are taken up by the child's own narrative productions. "Children's first narrative productions occur in action, in episodes of symbolic play by groups of peers, accompanied by – rather than solely though – language" (Nelson 2003: 28). Indeed, we should say they occur in *interaction* since we learn to form narratives through interactions with others – for example, when caregivers elicit the child's account of actions or events that have recently occurred by questions and prompts, and when young children around two to three years of age appropriate the narratives of others for their own (Nelson 2003).

Children further develop language and memory skills around three to four years of age and fine-tune their narrative abilities. Directly connected with their ability to pass false-belief tests, at around four years of age they start to represent the views of other people in their narratives, contrasting what they know about some events with what others know about the events (Perner 1992). Notably, narrative training has been shown to contribute to improved performances on false-belief tasks (Garfield, Peterson, & Perry 2001; Guajardo & Watson 2002). Accordingly, when capacities associated with primary and secondary intersubjectivity are integrated with newly acquired narrative capacities, young children are ready to understand things and people in emerging narrative structures. By engaging in such narrative practices, children learn to make sense of others as acting for reasons.

6.4 Sense-Making

Sense-making is a basic concept in enactive philosophy, and making sense of others, and *with* others, forms an essential part of sense-making in humans. We indicated that for autopoietic enactivism cognition is fully embodied and that the specific kind of body involved determines the structures and properties in the environment relevant to the organism's continued existence. An organism that meets the environment on its own sensorimotor terms brings forth or enacts what counts as a meaningful world (Thompson 2005: 418). "Exchanges with the world are inherently significant for the cognizer and this is the definitional property of a cognitive system: the creation and appreciation of meaning or sense-making in short" (Di Paolo, Rohde, & De Jaegher 2007). In this respect, cognition in humans with evolved brains and nervous systems, living in environments with others and with formed social structures, will be different from cognition in nonhuman animals. In humans, meaning emerges primarily through coordinated interaction with others.

Hanne De Jaegher and Ezequiel Di Paolo (2007) thus propose that within the human social context, intersubjective interaction involves "participatory sense-making" (PSM). "Meaning is generated and transformed in the interplay between the unfolding interaction process and the individuals engaged in it" (2007: 485). Participatory sense-making, in this sense, is closely related to the concept of secondary intersubjectivity. Participatory sense-making addresses the issue of how our intersubjective interactions enter into meaning constitution, and most generally the co-constitution of a meaningful world. It provides an answer to the question: How do we, together, interacting with each other, constitute the meaning of the world? According to De Jaegher and Di Paolo (2007) this addresses issues concerning social cognition, and helps to explain how we understand others given that we engage with them in a shared context formed by joint attention and joint action (secondary intersubjectivity). "This allows us to reframe the problem of social cognition as that of how meaning is generated and transformed in the interplay between the unfolding interaction process and the individuals engaged in it" (2007: 485). Specifically, the problem is reframed as one that cannot be solved in the standard terms of methodological individualism, where mechanisms within individuals, like mirror neurons or ToM modules, are appealed to as the primary explanation. Rather, processes of interaction, which extend beyond any individual involved, are taken as an important part of the explanation. Although social interaction involves the autonomy of each individual agent, it results in "emergent features in the collective dynamics that are not reducible to the sum of its parts" (Zhang et al. 2020: 11; see De Jaegher et al. 2010). The dynamical aspects of interaction, which depend on the participants' history of coordination, and contribute to the formation of an identifiable communicative pattern, will affect the way interactors understand each other.

> [W]hat arises in the process of coordination (e.g., gestures, utterances and changes in intonation that are sometimes labelled as back-channeling or turn-repair, etc.) can have the consequence of steering the encounter or facilitating (or not) its continuation. And the particular unravelling of these dynamics itself influences what kinds of coordination are more likely to happen. (De Jaegher & Di Paolo 2007: 492)

Ethnographic studies and conversation analysis support the role of inter-action dynamics in meaning-constituting encounters (e.g., Goodwin 2000). To capture the significance of these dynamics, one can employ a method of dynamical analysis proposed by Scott Kelso (2014) and his colleagues, called "coordination dynamics" (Tognoli et al. 2020; Tognoli & Kelso 2015). Although much of their work focuses on brain dynamics, their approach generalizes to any complex dynamical system and can apply to patterns of interaction which are typically bound together by coordination across different spatio-temporal scales (Kelso 2009; Zhang et al. 2020). The measuring of coordination dynamics by recording continuous time-varying processes as they unfold and then analyzing the dynamical structure of such processes using time-series analysis allow researchers to get into the fine details of the interactional processes and to develop explanatory models of how they are ordered. Subjects with autism spectrum disorder, for example, manifest signifi-cant differences in the coordination dynamics of communicative processes (Dumas, Kelso, & Nadel 2014; see Gallagher, Varga, & Sparaci 2022). More generally, "disordered social interactions play a pervasive role in many, if not all, psychiatric disorders" (Leong & Schilbach 2019: 636).

6.5 Complex Cognition

We mentioned that one promissory note issued by enactivism concerns the explanation of complex, or what is usually called "higher-order" cognition. This has been termed the "scaling-up" problem. Enactive approaches are said to be, at best, in a position to explain only lower-order or basic types of cognitive processes involving perception and action. But are they able to scale up to explain "representation-hungry," higher-order cognitive capabilities, such as memory, imagination, reflective judgment, and so on (e.g., Chemero 2009; Clowes & Mendonça 2016)?

Enactive theorists have proposed a number of different approaches to this issue, focused on imagination, mathematical cognition, and language (Gallagher 2017; Hutto, Kirchhoff, & Abrahamson 2015; Kiverstein & Rietveld 2021; Van Den Herik 2018; Zahidi & Myin 2016). The common strategy is to think of complex cognition as continuous with basic cognition, and as involving the same or similar skills. We can think of skills of conceptual analysis or rational problem-solving, for example, as involving the manipula-tion of affordances which may be of a conceptual or linguistic nature. Clearly, mathematical and scientific reasoning are examples of complex skillful know-how. Solving a problem in math, for example, means moving things around – for example, moving elements from one side of an equation to another, or constructing geometrical proofs by literally constructing figures and shapes. In this respect enactive approaches share an emphasis with extended cognition approaches on the use of tools and artifacts. Scientific cognition can also be seen as continuous with basic cognition, if we think of scientific models as material objects we can manipulate, conceptually, or even physically in extended material engagement (Rolla & Novaes 2022). In such cases, the representations are external ones, for example diagrams, charts, and figures, and the manipulations can be motoric or perceptual, setting one thing beside the other, turning it this way and that, viewing it by posing one question and then another, and so forth. This is an affordance-based process, understood "precisely in the ecological sense . . . . [of offering] possibilities of engagement. Exploring these possibilities is a matter of exercising sensorimotor abilities and exploring sensorimotor regularities" (Rolla & Novaes 2022: 631). We can gain scientific knowledge using a variety of equipment in labs or experimental settings. We can create simulations on the computer and manipulate them to discover results that we may not be able to grasp with unassisted thinking. Oftentimes we do our scientific exploration with others, presenting models and discussing them. In this regard, "models are somehow materialized inhabitants of the intersubjective field of human activity" (Knuuttila & Voutilainen 2003: 1487) – the product of participatory sense-making.

There is, of course, more to scientific cognition than manipulating models and the picking-up of affordances, as Rolla and Novaes acknowledge, "for science typically involves explanations, complex uses of language, very sophisticated inferences and so on" (2022: 627). Nonetheless, they argue for a continuum between basic and higher cognition. In this context they discuss the idea that someone learning about a planetary system may grasp something of its structure by coming to understand *how* orbits work, specifically by engaging with or manipulating a model, exploring its affordances and sensorimotor regularities. Indeed, this is shown in an experiment that employed what Robb Lindgren and I termed "enactive metaphors" (Gallagher & Lindgren 2015). In a project entitled "MEteor" we used a wall- and floor-projected dynamic simulation of planetary astronomy (planets with gravitational properties that support orbiting satellites, etc.). Middle-school children interact with MEteor by using their bodies (kicking and running) to launch an asteroid with a certain velocity and then predict where the asteroid will move in the context of other planets and associated forces. This involves an enactive metaphor in the sense that the child identifies with the meteor and acts out its behavior. Using MEteor, the children are guided through a progression of ideas and principles in the physics of how objects move in space (e.g., concepts of gravitational acceleration and Kepler's laws of planetary motion). Feedback about the child's ongoing predictions is delivered in real-time simulation prompts about adjusting trajectories.

To demonstrate the effectiveness of the whole-body enactive engagement for learning science concepts we compared a strong enactive condition (where children entered an immersive, room-sized simulated environment and moved their whole body to manipulate the meteor) to a weak enactive condition (where children manipulated the simulation on a computer screen using a computer mouse) in a set of controlled studies of 312 middle-school students (Lindgren & Bolling 2013; Lindgren & Moshell 2011). The strong enactive condition resulted in better understanding of astronomy concepts – production of more dynamical diagrams, less reliance on surface/background features of the simulation, and improvements in scientific reasoning on tests and dispositional learning effects.

One might think that this kind of simulation could be internalized and manipulated mentally. Indeed, enactive theorists have appealed to some version of internal imaginative simulation that would be more appropriate for proponents of weak EC. Evan Thompson (2007), for example, in explaining memory and imagination, tries to work out a nonrepresentational version of simulation as a re-enactment of perceptual processes. Memory, for example, may involve a (re-) activated presentational activity that evokes or brings to presence something that is absent. One objection is that even if one considers the original perceptual process to be nonrepresentational, the memory surely looks like a representation, although it could be considered as such only as a product that does not involve representational mechanisms in the production process itself. The simulation would be considered an emulation that "represents an activity by reenacting it in a circumscribed and modified way – for example, as an internal process that models but does not loop through the peripheral sensory and motor systems" (Thompson 2007: 290–291).

This still seems uncomfortably close to a representationalist explanation. Too close for Daniel Hutto, who is more suspicious of the emulator concept since it is too frequently conceived in terms of representational content. For Hutto's radical view (REC), it would be a defeat for enactivist accounts "if emulators are part of the best explanation of mental imagery and the detailed account of how they work turns out to involve the manipulation of representational contents" (Hutto 2015: 72). He suggests that the enactive account has to stay closer to the processes involved in the event that is remembered or imagined. Rather than scale up to complex processes, one should scale down those processes to more basic ones. In this respect we can start to think about ways that memory and imagination are already involved in perception and action. Hutto appeals to the example of Middle Paleolithic hominin toolmaking capacities in working with stone flakes to form instruments. This is a type of material engagement that requires a close integration of memory, perhaps in the form of motor habit, and imagination, in the form of anticipating the finished product – both of which are required to keep track of the process that is being conducted by the hands. In this practice, seeing, remembering, and imagining are all tightly integrated, and, as in the case of many skills, there is not much one can provide in terms of descriptions of how to do it; there is nothing like content or a set of rules that can be explicated discursively. Nor is there need for something like an internal representation of the stone. The stone is at hand, the stone-knapper can feel it, and can see what to do in the specifics of its size, shape, and weight. The mental processes, the perception, the imagination, the memory, are integrated with the action of forming the tool. In this material engagement (Malafouris 2013), the hands are not isolated from the brain, nor from the objects that they manipulate.

This could count as a starting point from which one would need to build up such basic memory and imaginative processes into the more complex forms of cognition. One could argue for a continuity from the basic to the complex. One could also argue that in the human case, language, communication, and narrative practices push or bootstrap such basic cognitive processes into new and more complex accomplishments. Given the considerations about social interaction and participatory sense-making outlined in the previous sections, enactivists are already in a position to offer an account of cognitive practices that are more complex than perception and action.

I'll conclude this section by reviewing once again the challenge questions, now posed to enactivism.

1. *Which notion of embodiment is operative?* Enactive EC, like strong EC, emphasizes that the cognitive system is brain–body–environment, where body includes the full nonneural organism understood in action-oriented, dynamical relation to its environments.
2. *Which sectors of cognition or which cognitive tasks are embodied, and how fully does each task involve embodiment?* Perception and action are treated as basic cognitive processes that scale up to more complex forms of sense-making via intersubjective (social and cultural) practices.
3. *What empirical evidence supports specific embodiment claims?* Dynamical analysis of brain–body–environment systems have been supported by experimental work in neurobiology and various psychological disciplines. Enactive approaches also draw on developmental, ethnographic, and phenomenological studies.
4. *How do the proffered claims depart substantially from CC?* Enactive EC emphasizes the role of body–environment interactions and rejects models

that are primarily computational, representational, and information-theoretic.

5. *What role do mental or neural representations play in cognition?* Enactive EC endorses nonrepresentational approaches; REC highlights the hard problem of content and rejects representational explanations.

7 Causation, Constitution, and Free Energy

In this section I return to some loose ends that need to be tied and tidied up. First, I'll consider the strongest objection to both extended and enactive EC, the so-called causation/coupling-constitution fallacy (mentioned in Section 5.1), and how extended and enactive EC may make common cause to defend against it. Second, I'll consider the viability of ongoing attempts to consolidate extended and enactive approaches by integrating them in a PP framework that focuses on the free-energy principle.

7.1 The C-C Fallacy

In line with the original objection to the EMH (Adams & Aizawa 2001), several philosophers (Aizawa 2007; Block 2005; Prinz 2006) have suggested that enactive approaches also conflate claims about causal contribution with claims about constitution (the C-C fallacy). For example, Gangopadhyay and Kiverstein (2009) consider sensory-motor contingencies, like those expressed in eye movements during perception, to be partly constitutive of perception, rather than simply causal factors. Specifically, they argue that such movements are part of what constitutes perceptual attention. That is, attention, as a cognitive operation, just is a way of coupling to the environment that is embodied in eye movements that are correlated to task.

> If the capacity to perform eye movements is impaired this disrupts the lawlike relationships between input and output that determine perceptual content. This disruption occurs at the level of the perceiver's sensorimotor coupling with the environment. Its profound effect on perceptual content establishes that sensorimotor behaviour can make a truly constitutive contribution to the contents of experience. (Gangopadhyay & Kiverstein 2009: 72)

Others take a similar tack, allowing for the causal–constitutive distinction, but arguing, based on empirical evidence, that embodied engagements are constitutive for cognition since embodied sensorimotor and cognitive processes are inseparable, and that without such body–environment coupling, some aspect of the cognitive process would be unavailable to us (e.g., Clark 2008a). This argument is not always convincing to the critics since they understand coupling to be a causal relation rather than a constitutive one (e.g., Adams & Aizawa 2010).

A more incisive response to the C-C fallacy claim is to show that the distinction between causal and constitutive relations is not as strict as the critics think. In this respect, enactive responses have defended a conception of constitution that involves a specific kind of causality. To see this, we should first note that the causality–constitution distinction appealed to by Adams and Aizawa is derived from the new-mechanist literature (e.g., Bechtel & Huang 2022; Craver 2007; Craver & Bechtel 2007). The concept of constitution operative in such mechanist theories is compositional. That is, it can be defined mereologically in terms of parts that synchronically or contemporaneously make up (constitute) a whole. On one level, the parts work together causally under certain background conditions, but the higher-order composition emerges noncausally. Lower-level properties can realize higher-order properties, and lower-level processes can implement higher-order processes. This kind of compositional inter-level constitution of a macro phenomenon at a higher level is noncausal, even if it involves productive intra-level mechanistic-causal processes at the lower level. Thus, causal relations are *intra*-level relations only; constitutive relations are *inter*-level noncausal relations (Figure 1).

The diagram shows components X1–X4 at the lower level engaging in causal processes (φ1-ing – φ4-ing); these components constitute S; the lower-order processes noncausally implement the higher-order process (ψ-ing). According to Aizawa (2014: 24), we can think of the mechanism as a whole signifying "something like" a person solving a problem (S ψ-ing). He suggests, φ1-ing – φ4-ing could signify subpersonal neural processes or even subpersonal non-neural processes: "X1φ1-ing might be the eye performing a saccade, where X4φ4-ing might be writing with a pencil."

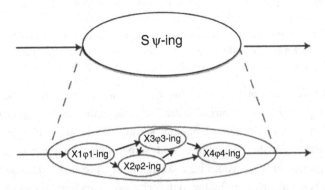

Figure 1 Schema of mechanism (redrawn from Craver 2007: 7)

There are two reasons why new-mechanist theorists such as Craver and Bechtel distinguish between causality and constitution.

1. The relation between part and whole cannot be causal, because causality involves mereological independence of cause and effect. For example, the handle of the teacup is part of the teacup, but it does not cause the teacup.
2. Part–whole relations must be contemporaneous relations; causality requires diachronicity.

A problem with this strict distinction arises when Craver proposes mutual manipulability (MM) as a criterion that tests for constitutive relations.

> My working account of constitutive relevance is as follows: a component is relevant to the behavior of a mechanism as a whole when one can wiggle the behavior of the whole by wiggling the behavior of the component and one can wiggle the behavior of the component by wiggling the behavior as a whole. The two are related as part and whole and they are mutually manipulable. (Craver 2007: 152–153)

The problem is that Craver explains the notion of whole–part mutual wiggling in terms of James Woodward's (2003) interventionist conception of causality. But this seems to introduce causality into the constitution relation. Mutual manipulability, as defined on the notion of Woodwardian intervention, would pick out causal relations, but inter-level constitutional relations are not supposed to be causal. This complication has motivated a debate within the new-mechanist literature that we don't need to rehearse here. It's enough to point out that at least one attempt to resolve the confusion has been to allow for inter-level causal relations by introducing the realistic assumption that the higher-level constituted phenomenon (S ψ-ing) is itself diachronic, so that an early lower-level process might in fact be causally related to a later higher-order process (Krickel 2018). Accordingly, an intervention on one lower-level process, $X1\varphi1$-ing, for example, may wiggle, not the whole mechanism, but a temporal part of the S ψ-ing that is diachronically later than $X1\varphi1$-ing. This motivates the idea of a diachronic conception of constitution which would be perfectly consistent with the test of MM (Kirchhoff 2017).

This diachronic view fits well with an enactivist dynamical conception of constitution. To the extent that a cognitive process involves an organism engaging with its environment, the active system is constituted through processes of dynamical coupling, involving causal relations that are not simply linear, or reciprocal, but, in addition, involve dynamical nonlinear causality where the whole can recursively influence the working of the part. Such causal relations may include elements, properties, relations, and processes that are not internal to the organism, or reducible to just the organism. Coupling is indeed causal, but just those coupling relations are constitutive of the cognitive processes which are distributed across different time-scales of brain–body–environment (Varela 1999). Anthony Chemero (2009) and Orestis Palermos (2014) argue that the presence of just such nonlinear relations, or the continuous mutual interaction loops which entail such causal relations, counts as an objective criterion of constitution. In effect, enactivism redefines constitution in a way that makes it immune to the C-C fallacy.

7.2 The Free-Energy Principle and Enaction

We saw in Section 5.3 a proposed alliance between extended cognition and predictive processing. Isn't it possible to integrate PP accounts and enactivism, as some have suggested (Bruineberg, Kiverstein, & Rietveld 2018; Gallagher & Allen 2018; Kiverstein 2020; Parr, Da Costa, & Friston 2020; Wiese & Friston 2021)? This clearly involves addressing some terminological and conceptual differences concerning neurocentric internalism and the concepts of inference, internal model, and representation (Ramstead et al. 2021). Is it possible for PP to accommodate enactivist processes of affordance, attunement, and resonance without undermining its own principles?

Constant, Clark, and Friston (2021), in their article on "representation wars," do think it is possible. They propose a truce that would introduce a division of labor. "[There] is a subtle, yet crucial point, which becomes apparent when considering the probability distributions involved in various inference processes in the brain" (2021: n.p.). Here they make the distinction between (1) the brain predicting expected sensory neural activations matching the probability of the generative model/belief – a purely internal process – and (2) the brain's prediction about the (hidden) cause of such activations. "Getting it right" (fulfilling truth or success conditions) in the case of (1) "is about getting it right with respect to one's own beliefs; e.g., successfully exploring the state space of one's own model of the world . . . . This means that under active inference, there are two layers of success involved, one defined over the model, and one defined over the agent-world coupling" (2021: n.p.).

According to Constant et al., the first type of PP is representational and fits well with prediction error minimization; the second is dynamical and modeled on active inference or enactive processes. They explain that the second (non-representational) process is sufficient for deontic actions – actions guided by normative constraints, which for them includes habitual actions approaching automatic behavior. They give the example of stopping at stop signs, which drivers tend to do automatically.

[Such actions] do not have success conditions *qua* brain processes, but rather have success conditions *qua* agent-world coupling processes. They are simple observation-action loops; not rich and reconstructive policy selection loops ... . inferences about states of the world – that admit a representationalist interpretation – are now replaced by direct action, without any intervening inference or representation of the consequences of action. (2021: n.p.)

With respect to deontic actions, what does the work is "a kind of perceptually maintained motor-informational grip on the world: a low-cost perception-action routine that retrieves the right information just-in-time for use, and that is not in the business of building up a rich inner simulacrum" (Clark 2015: 11).

Although Constant et al. (2021) pitch this as a kind of détente, it's not clear how it moves beyond older peace negotiations that involved splitting the difference between higher-order representation-hungry cognition (albeit now framed in PP terms) and more basic perceptual-motor processes (e.g., Clark & Toribio 1994). It's also not clear how enactive, heedful, or intelligent habit fits this picture, since even with respect to perception-action loops, enactive processes are not a matter of automatic, repetitive deontic behavior.

Another attempt at integrating PP and enactive approaches is made by stepping back from some of these details into a more basic and abstract framework. As already noted (in Section 6.2), for Friston the important thing is getting the mathematics (in the statistical models) right, and this informs his proposal to generalize his model to life itself explained in terms of the free-energy principle (FEP).[8] According to FEP, and the second law of thermodynamics, biological systems are defined by the tendency to resist entropy; to do otherwise would entail systemic death. To maintain homeostasis and structural and functional integrity, and to avoid entropy (which in thermodynamic terms means too much free energy in the system), then the organism should reduce free energy (the corollary of which is to minimize prediction errors and surprisal in the PP model) via active inference – that is, by changing its relation to the environment. The claim is that, in some regards, FEP aligns well with the concept of autopoiesis, the emergent or self-organizing persistence of an organism in virtue of its own dynamical structure. Both principles express the continuous processes of life and mind (Allen & Friston 2018; Ramstead et al. 2021).

---

[8] See Friston (2013). According to FEP, self-organizing organisms resist the natural tendency to entropy implied by the second law of thermodynamics, in order to "maintain their states and form in the face of a constantly changing environment" (Friston 2010). Kirchhoff and Froese (2017: 1) characterize FEP as follows: "organisms act to maintain themselves in their expected biological and cognitive states ... they can do so only by minimizing their free energy given that the long-term average of free energy is entropy."

The strategy here, to put it simply, is that if FEP and autopoiesis can be understood to be consistent, then there is a good basis for integrating PP and enactivism. Some enactivists agree that we can mesh the basic FEP version of predictive active inference models with enactivist principles (e.g., Bruineberg, Kiverstein, & Rietveld 2018; Kirchhoff 2018; Kirchhoff & Froese 2017). They emphasize the embodied action (active inference) that the organism can use to control its own viability conditions.

> So within the free-energy framework, it is *action* that does the work of actually minimizing surprisal. Actions change an organism's relation to the environment, thereby changing the sensory states of the organism. (Bruineberg et al. 2018)

According to Kirchhoff and Froese, a particular version of FEP supports the nonrepresentationalist, radical enactive view of cognition (REC):

> [A]ssuming that information-as-covariance cannot give rise to information-as-content, and assuming that responding adaptively to information-as-covariance is an essential property of living and cognitive systems, then mentality is not in its most basic forms a matter of processing any kind of [representational] content. (2017: 13).

On this view, action is not something that happens in the brain; it's not just providing new sensory input for neural processing, but is rather what the whole organism does in its interactions with the environment or, under a different description, what a person does in the world, and this changes the world as much as it changes the brain. The system priors – that is, the prior knowledge that informs action – are not (just) assumptions or beliefs that inform inferences; they includes the know-how of embodied skills, patterns of action-readiness, and affective dispositions that mesh with an affordance space.

In contrast to attempts to integrate PP and enactivist approaches, Di Paolo, Thompson, and Beer (2022) identify some deeper (technical and theoretical) reasons why PP is not compatible with enaction. To put this in its simplest terms, the technical part of the argument involves contrasting autopoietic systems with FEP systems. In autopoietic systems *organization*, as an invariable, is distinguished from *structure*, as a changeable feature – a distinction not maintained in the FEP discussion.

> The structure is the system's actual realization, the concrete components that constitute a system and the actual and concrete relations between them. The system's organization is the abstract set of relations that define the system as belonging to a class. Autopoiesis is the description of a class of systems, i.e., a description of the organization that defines this class. Concrete autopoietic systems may be instantiated in a wide variety of structures, and a given

structure may belong to more than one class of organization . . . . Structures also change over time, even if the organization remains invariant. (Di Paolo, Thompson, & Beer 2022: 12)

Organization and structure signify two different kinds of homeostasis. According to the FEP, homeostasis refers to structure (the structural integrity of a system); according to autopoietic theory, homeostasis refers to organization. In an autopoietic system, processes undergo transformation in order to regenerate the conditions of that system's own production; in an FEP system, there is no regeneration involved after the initial event – the system simply endures. "It is unclear in what sense the components of the systems . . . are *produced* by other processes in the system, instead of just being there by assumption" (Di Paolo, Thompson, & Beer 2022: 13). Accordingly, there is confusion when FEP systems are equated with autopoietic ones.

Di Paolo, Thompson, and Beer (2022: 24) also note the importance of the enactive system's history (its "historicity"). They make this last point more generally in terms of contrasting conceptions of brain dynamics (hierarchical comparators in PP, versus enactive conceptions of dynamical "history-dependence [even] in the most basic neuroscientific scenario of stimulus processing"). This point has implications for understanding development, plasticity, skill acquisition, habit formation, and the ability to be cognitively flexible and creative.

Indeed, one way to cash out these theoretical incommensurabilities in pragmatic terms is to consider examples of creativity, novelty, or improvisation. In this regard, Philipp Schwartenbek et al. phrase the question in just the right way.

If our main objective [on predictive models] is to minimize surprise over the states and outcomes we encounter, how can this explain complex human behavior such as novelty seeking, exploration, and, furthermore, higher level aspirations such as art, music, poetry, or humor? (Schwartenbeck et al. 2013: n.p.)

Schwartenbek et al., however, rather than focusing on art, music, poetry, or humor, focus on economic decision-making, explained in terms of exploring alternatives to fixed goal states known to have the highest expected utility. Referencing Schwartenbeck et al., Andy Clark (2018) addresses the problem directly, admitting, as Schwartenbeck et al. themselves do, that FEP does not provide a good account of creative, novel, or improvised action that may not be defined by fixed goals.

These prediction-error-minimizing agents exhibit at most a modest and instrumentally-motivated tendency towards play, exploration, and the search for novel experiences. These prediction error minimizing agents remain locked, it seems, into an information-theoretic journey whose guiding principle is in some way unacceptably conservative. It is a journey which, if successful, will be marked only by the attainment of expected goals and meta-goals. (Clark 2018: 528).

Likewise, as previously suggested, enactive processes are not well captured by the notion of deontic action, as characterized by Constant, Clark, and Friston (2021), that is, as unthinking or automatic, normatively guided action. Deontic action, as they understand it, clearly does not allow for innovation or impro-visation (Gallagher 2022).

To account for creativity, Clark appeals to environmental and cultural factors, "ecologically unique, self-engineered contexts of culture, technology, and lin-guaform exchange." Still, as he acknowledges, such factors may also limit possibilities for creativity and novelty.

> The skilled pianist has learnt to reduce prediction error with respect to complex melodies and motor repertoires, and the skilled mathematician with respect to properties and relations among numbers, theorems, and other constructs. But the musical and mathematical traditions within which they operate reflect the operation of cultural forces such as practices of writing, reflecting, disseminating, and peer review. (Clark 2018: 531)

Clark argues, however, that it could go either way – environment and cultural practices may provide limits to, or (somehow) may enable creativity. The question remains, how does a practice work when it enables creativity?[9] And then, almost as if on cue, he suggests: "These powerful effects are further explored in work by 'enactivists' sympathetic to PP – for example, Rietveld and Kiverstein (2014), Bruineberg et al. (2018), Gallagher et al. (2013)" (2018: 531). That seems exactly right; indeed, the focus on embodiment, affect, and environmental coupling, actually pushes us away from PP and toward more enactive accounts, a point reiterated by Di Paolo, Thompson, and Beer.

> [Thus], phenomena such as developmental spurts in skill level signal changes in dynamical configurations (novel constraints, emergent parameters, chan-ging variable sets). The variability entailed in changing dynamical configur-ations has been postulated as the origin of motor creativity . . . the very idea of which is rendered problematic without an account of historical change. (Di Paolo, Thompson, & Beer 2022: 23).

Motor creativity, for example, essential in the performing arts, reflects the history and skill of the agent. On the enactive view, performers, based on their

---

[9] Michael Wheeler (2018) provides an insightful answer to this question that builds on 3E cognition (embodied, embedded, and extended), and that emphasizes the role that cognitive niches and external contexts play in fostering creativity. His explanation makes no mention of either PP or enactivism, although I would argue it is fully consistent with enactivist views.

well-trained skills and well-formed habits (which involve a heedful flexibility rather than automaticity or repetitiveness) are able to move beyond controlled engagement to the point of not-knowing (embracing a kind of uncertainty or surprise) about what precisely will happen – letting the system (brain–body–environment) move in unpredictable, surprising ways – without a prediction of what happens next. What happens next, on the enactive view, is that brain–body–environment couple in novel ways – they join forces to enact something unpredictable – they create cortical patterns, and behaviors, and new affordances that are unique to each event.

8 Conclusion: Some Practical Implications and Applications

Studies of creativity and improvisational performance in the arts have recently been reframed by approaches that champion 4E cognition. These include studies of music (Høffding 2019; Krueger 2014; Ryan & Gallagher 2020; Schiavio & Høffding 2015; Van Der Schyff et al. 2018); dance (He & Ravn 2018; Merritt 2015; Ravn 2016; Ravn & Høffding 2021); theater and film (Gallagher & Gallagher 2020; Gallese & Guerra 2012; Sutton & Tribble 2011; Tribble 2011). The study of performance, however, is just one area that has seen the impact of EC. To conclude, let me briefly highlight some other areas (beyond the cognitive sciences) where EC approaches have emerged or have gained significant influence.

- In the field of *education* there have been some general interventions (Hutto & Abrahamson 2022; Skulmowski & Rey 2018 provide a good review), and some very specific interventions in, for example, the use of virtual reality and full-body immersion in learning science concepts (Gallagher & Lindgren 2015), as well as studies supporting, for example, language learning (Aden & Eschenauer 2020), and mathematics education (Abrahamson & Sánchez-García 2016; Hutto, Kirchhoff, & Abrahamson 2015; Soto-Andrade 2018).
- *Literature and the humanities.* There is a growing body of work in this area, spurred on by recent international conferences and edited volumes on EC, distributed cognition, and historical literary studies (Anderson 2015; Anderson, Wheeler, & Sprevak 2019; Cave 2017).
- *Architecture.* The reorganization of space is not only captured in the objective measurements of the architectural structures of the built environment, but also in a way that modulates the lived body and the way that space is experienced. As Mark Johnson writes, in regard to architecture and embodied action, "we live in and through our ongoing interactions with environments that are both physical and cultural. The structures we make are loosely adapted to the functions we perform .... [We] order our environments to

enhance meaning in our lives and to open up possibilities for deepened and enriched experience" (2015: 33; also see, for example, Jäger, Schnädelbach, & Hale 2016; Jelić et al. 2016; Rietveld & Brouwers 2017).

- *Economics.* Embodied approaches to economic reasoning have made use of the EMH (Clark 1996) and, in the context of institutional economics, enactive and extended views on how cognitive institutions work (Gallagher, Mastrogiorgio, & Petracca 2019; Oullier & Basso 2010; Petracca 2021; Petracca & Gallagher 2020)

- *Psychiatry and clinical reasoning.* Embodied and enactive approaches emphasize the integration of the various processes and factors, including social and cultural factors, that contribute to different patterns of psychiatric disorders (de Haan 2020; Gallagher 2023). These approaches also have implications for psychotherapeutic practices (Fuchs & Röhricht 2017; Hutto & Gallagher 2017; Koch, Caldwell, & Fuchs 2013; Röhricht et al. 2014).

- *Medicine and physical therapy.* EC contributes to rethinking clinical reasoning in the context of physical therapy (Halák & Kříž 2022; Øberg, Normann, & Gallagher 2015), and emphasizes the importance of organism–environment coupling in medical practice and education (Costa-Cordella, Reardon, & Parada 2022).

In all of these areas EC tends to challenge existing paradigms. These applications are helpful for sorting out the practical implications of EC theory, and from the EC perspective these are important projects that loop back to inform the ongoing development of 4E theory.

References

Abrahamson, D. & Sánchez-García, R. (2016). Learning is moving in new ways: The ecological dynamics of mathematics education. *Journal of the Learning Sciences*, **25(2), 203–239**.

Adams, F. & Aizawa, K. (2001). The bounds of cognition. *Philosophical Psychology*, **14(1), 43–64**.

Adams, F. & Aizawa, K. (2010). Defending the bounds of cognition. In R. Menary (ed.), *The Extended Mind*. Cambridge, MA: MIT Press, pp. **67–80**.

Aden, J. & Eschenauer, S. (2020). Translanguaging: An enactive-performative approach to language education. In E. Moore, J. Bradley, & J. Simpson (eds.), *Translanguaging as Transformation: The Collaborative Construction of New Linguistic Realities*. Berlin: De Gruyter, pp. **102–117**.

Aizawa, K. (2007). Understanding the embodiment of perception. *The Journal of Philosophy*, **104(1), 5–25**.

Aizawa, K. (2014). The enactivist revolution. *Avant*, **(5)2, 1–24**. **DOI**: http://doi.org/10.12849/50202014.0109.0002.

Akins, K. (1996). Of sensory systems and the "aboutness" of mental states. *The Journal of Philosophy*, **93(7), 337–372**.

Allen, M. & Friston, K. J. (2018). From cognitivism to autopoiesis: Towards a computational framework for the embodied mind. *Synthese*, **195(6), 2459–2482**.

Alsmith, A. J. T. & de Vignemont, F. (2012). Embodying the mind and representing the body. *Review of Philosophy and Psychology*, **3(1), 1–13**.

Alviar, C., Kello, C. T., & Dale, R. (2023). Multimodal coordination and pragmatic modes in conversation. *Language Sciences* 97, 101524. DOI: https://doi.org/10.1016/j.langsci.2022.101524.

Anderson, M. (2015). *The Renaissance Extended Mind*. London: Palgrave Macmillan. London

Anderson, M., Wheeler, M., & Sprevak, M. (2019). Distributed cognition and the humanities. In M. Anderson, D. Cairns, & M. Sprevak (eds.), *Distributed Cognition in Medieval and Renaissance Culture*. Edinburgh: Edinburgh University Press, pp. **1–17**.

Anderson, M. L. (2010). Neural reuse: A fundamental organizational principle of the brain. *Behavioral and Brain Sciences*, **33(4), 245–266**.

Andres, M., Seron, X., & Olivier, E. (2007). Contribution of hand motor circuits to counting. *Journal of Cognitive Neuroscience*, **19(4), 563–576**.

Astington, J. (1990). Narrative and the child's theory of mind. In B. K. Britton & D. Pellegrini (eds.), *Narrative Thought and Narrative Language*. Hillsdale, NJ: Erlbaum, pp. **151–171**.

Baillargeon, R., Scott, R. M., & Bian, L. (2016). Psychological reasoning in infancy. *Annual Review of Psychology*, **67, 159–186**.

Baron-Cohen, S. (1997). *Mindblindness: An Essay on Autism and Theory of Mind*. Cambridge, MA: MIT Press.

Barsalou, L. W. (1999). Perceptual symbol systems. *Behavioral and Brain Sciences*, **22, 577–660**.

Barsalou, L. W. (2008). Grounded cognition. *Annual Review of Psychology*, **59, 617–645**.

Bechtel, W., & Huang, L. T. L. (2022). *Philosophy of Neuroscience*. Cambridge: Cambridge University Press.

Beer, R. (2000). Dynamical approaches to cognitive science. *Trends in Cognitive Sciences*, **4, 91–99**.

Berlucchi, G. & Aglioti, S. M. (2010). The body in the brain revisited. *Experimental Brain Research*, **200(1), 25–35**.

Berthoz, A. (2000). *The Brain's Sense of Movement*. Cambridge, MA: Harvard University Press.

Block, N. (2005). Review of Alva Noe: *Action in Perception. Journal of Philosophy*, **102(5), 259–272**.

Bower, M. & Gallagher, S. (2013). Bodily affectivity: Prenoetic elements in enactive perception. *Phenomenology and Mind*, **2, 108–131**.

Bredo, E. (1994). Reconstructing educational psychology: Situated cognition and Deweyan pragmatism. *Educational Psychologist*, **29, 23–35**.

Brooks, R. (1991). Intelligence without representation. *Artificial Intelligence*, **47, 139–159**.

Bruineberg, J., Kiverstein, J., & Rietveld, E. (2018). The anticipating brain is not a scientist: The free-energy principle from an ecological-enactive perspective. *Synthese*, **195(6), 2417–2444**.

Burge, T. (2010). Origins of perception. Paper presented as the First 2010 Jean Nicod Prize Lecture, Paris, June 14, 2010.

Buttelmann, D., Carpenter, M. & Tomasello, M. (2009). Eighteen-month-old infants show false belief understanding in an active helping paradigm. *Cognition*, **112(2), 337–342**.

Caligiuri, M. P. & Ellwanger, J. (2000). Motor and cognitive aspects of motor retardation in depression. *Journal of Affective Disorders*, **57(1–3), 83–93**.

Carruthers, P. (2013). Mindreading in infancy. *Mind & Language*, **28(2), 141–172**.

Casasanto, D. & Dijkstra, K. (2010). Motor action and emotional memory. *Cognition*, **115(1), 179–185**.

Cash, M. (2013). Cognition without borders: "Third wave" socially distributed cognition and relational autonomy. *Cognitive Systems Research*, **25–26, 61–71**.

Cave, T. (2017). Situated cognition: The literary archive. *Poetics Today*, **38(2), 235–253**.

Chemero, A. (2001). Dynamical explanation and mental representations. *Trends in Cognitive Sciences*, **5(4), 141–142**.

Chemero, A. (2009). *Radical Embodied Cognitive Science*. Cambridge, MA: MIT Press.

Chen, S. & Bargh, J. A. (1999). Consequences of automatic evaluation: Immediate behavior predispositions to approach or avoid the stimulus. *Personality and Social Psychology Bulletin*, **25, 215–224**.

Chiel, H. & Beer, R. (1997). The brain has a body: Adaptive behavior emerges from interactions of nervous system, body and environment. *Trends in Neuroscience*, **20, 553–557**.

Chomsky, N. (1995). Language and nature. *Mind*, **104, 1–61**.

Churchland, P. S., Ramachandran, V. S., & Sejnowski, T. J. (1994). A critique of pure vision. In C. Koch & J. L. Davis (eds.), *Large-Scale Neuronal Theories of the Brain*. Cambridge, MA: MIT Press.

Cisek, P. & Kalaska, J. F. (2010). Neural mechanisms for interacting with a world full of action choices. *Annual Review of Neuroscience*, **33, 269–298**.

Clapin, H. (2002). *The Philosophy of Mental Representation*. Oxford: Oxford University Press.

Clark, A. (1996). Economic reason: The interplay of individual learning and external structure. In J. Drobak & J. Nye (eds.), *The Frontiers of the New Institutional Economics*. Bingley: Emerald Group Academic Publishers, pp. **269–270**.

Clark, A. (1997). *Being There*. Cambridge, MA: MIT Press.

Clark, A. (1999). An embodied cognitive science? *Trends in Cognitive Sciences*, **3(9), 345–351**.

Clark, A. (2008a). *Supersizing the Mind: Reflections on Embodiment, Action, and Cognitive Extension*. Oxford: Oxford University Press.

Clark, A. (2008b). Pressing the flesh: A tension on the study of the embodied, embedded mind. *Philosophy and Phenomenological Research*, **76, 37–59**.

Clark, A. (2010a). Memento's revenge: The extended mind, extended. In R. Menary (ed.), *The Extended Mind*. Cambridge, MA: MIT Press, pp. **43–66**.

Clark, A. (2010b). Coupling, constitution, and the cognitive kind: A reply to Adams and Aizaway. In R. Menary (ed.), *The Extended Mind*. Cambridge, MA: MIT Press, pp. **81–100**.

Clark, A. (2013). Whatever next? Predictive brains, situated agents, and the future of cognitive science. *Behavioral and Brain Sciences*, **36(3), 181–204**.

Clark, A. (2015). Radical predictive processing. *The Southern Journal of Philosophy*, **53(S1), 3–27**.

Clark, A. (2016). *Surfing uncertainty: Prediction, Action, and the Embodied Mind*. Oxford: Oxford University Press.

Clark, A. (2018). A nice surprise? Predictive processing and the active pursuit of novelty. *Phenomenology and the Cognitive Sciences*, **17(3), 521–534**.

Clark, A. & Chalmers, D. (1998). The extended mind. *Analysis*, **58(1), 7–19**.

Clark, A. & Grush, R. (1999). Towards a cognitive robotics. *Adaptive Behavior*, **7(1), 5–16**.

Clark, A. & Toribio, J. (1994). Doing without representing? *Synthese*, **101(3), 401–431**.

Clowes, R. W. & Mendonca, D. (2016). Representation redux: Is there still a useful role for representation to play in the context of embodied, dynamicist and situated theories of mind? *New Ideas in Psychology*, **40, 26–47**.

Colombetti, G. (2014). *The Feeling Body: Affective Science Meets the Enactive Mind*. Cambridge, MA: MIT Press.

Constant, A., Clark, A., & Friston, K. J. (2021). Representation wars: Enacting an armistice through active inference. *Frontiers in Psychology*, **11, 3798**.

Cosmelli, D. & Thompson, E. (2007). Embodiment or envatment? Reflections on the bodily basis of consciousness. In J. Stewart, O. Gapenne, & E. di Paolo (eds.), *Enaction: Towards a New Paradigm for Cognitive Science*. Cambridge, MA: MIT Press, pp. **361–386**.

Costa-Cordella, S., Reardon, E., & Parada, F. J. (**2022**). Towards a 4E perspective curricula for health and medical education. *PsyArXiv*, January 31, 2022. arXiv: http://doi.org/10.31234/osf.io/p2nqm.

Crane, T. (2008). Is perception a propositional attitude? *The Philosophical Quarterly*, **59 (236), 452–469**.

Craver, C. F. (2007). *Explaining the Brain: Mechanisms and the Mosaic Unity of Neuroscience*. New York: Oxford University Press.

Craver, C. F. & Bechtel, W. (2007). Top-down causation without top-down causes. *Biology and Philosophy*, **22, 547–63**.

Csibra, G. & Gergely, G. (2009). Natural pedagogy. *Trends in Cognitive Sciences*, **13, 148–153**.

Dale, R., Dietrich, E., & Chemero, A. (2009). Explanatory pluralism in cognitive science. *Cognitive Science*, **33(5)**, 739–42.

Damasio, A. (1994). *Descartes' Error: Emotion, Reason, and the Human Brain.* New York: G. P. Putnam.

Danziger, S., Levav, J., & Avnaim-Pesso, L. (2011). Extraneous factors in judicial decisions. *Proceedings of the National Academy of Sciences*, **108 (17), 6889–6892.**

Degenaar, J. & O'Regan, J. K. (2017). Sensorimotor theory and enactivism. *Topoi*, **36(3), 393–407.**

de Haan, S. (2020). *Enactive Psychiatry.* Cambridge: Cambridge University Press.

De Jaegher, H. & Di Paolo, E. (2007). Participatory sense-making: An enactive approach to social cognition. *Phenomenology and the Cognitive Sciences*, **6, 485–507.**

De Jaegher, H., Di Paolo, E., & Gallagher, S. (2010). Can social interaction constitute social cognition? *Trends in Cognitive Sciences*, **14(10), 441–447.**

Dennett, D. (1969). *Content and Consciousness.* London: Routledge.

Dewey, J. (1916). *Essays in Experimental Logic.* Chicago: University of Chicago Press.

Di Paolo, E. A. (2005). Autopoiesis, adaptivity, teleology, agency. *Phenomenology and the Cognitive Sciences*, **4, 97–125.**

Di Paolo, E. A., Rohde, M., & De Jaegher, H. (2007). Horizons for the enactive mind: Values, social interaction, and play. In J. Stewart, O. Gapenne, & E. Di Paolo (eds.), *Enaction: Towards a New Paradigm for Cognitive Science.* Cambridge, MA: MIT Press, pp. **33–88.**

Di Paolo, E., Thompson, E., & Beer, R. (2022). Laying down a forking path: Tensions between enaction and the free energy principle. *Philosophy and the Mind Sciences*, **3(2), 1–39.**

Dreyfus, H. L. (ed.) (1982). *Husserl, Intentionality, and Cognitive Science.* Cambridge, MA: MIT Press.

Dumas, G., Kelso, J. A., & Nadel, J. (2014). Tackling the social cognition paradox through multi-scale approaches. *Frontiers in Psychology*, **5, 882.**

Dunn, J. (1991). Understanding others: Evidence from naturalistic studies of children. In A. Whiten, ed., *Natural Theories of Mind: Evolution, Development and Simulation of Everyday Mindreading.* Oxford: Basil Blackwell, pp. **51–61.**

Egan, F. (2014). How to think about mental content. *Philosophical Studies*, **170, 115–135.**

Feldman, C. F., Bruner, J., Renderer, B., & Spitzer, S. (1990). Narrative comprehension. In B. K. Britton & A. D. Pellegrini (eds.), *Narrative Thought and Narrative Language*. Hillsdale, NJ: Lawrence Erlbaum Associates, pp. 1–78.

Findlay, J. M. & Gilchrist, I. D. (2003) *Active Vision: The Psychology of Looking and Seeing*. Oxford: Oxford University Press.

Fink, P. W., Foo, P. S., & Warren, W. H. (2009). Catching fly balls in virtual reality: A critical test of the outfielder problem. *Journal of Vision*, **9(13)**, 1–8.

Fiore, S. M., Salas, E., Cuevas, H. M., & Bowers, C. A. (2003). Distributed coordination space: Toward a theory of distributed team process and performance. *Theoretical Issues in Ergonomics Science*, **4(3–4)**, 340–364.

Fodor, J. A. (2008). *LOT 2: The Language of Thought Revisited*. Oxford: Oxford University Press.

Fogel, A. & Thelen, E. (1987). Development of early expressive and communicative action: Reinterpreting the evidence from a dynamic systems perspective. *Developmental Psychology*, **23(6), 747**.

Friston, K. (2013). Life as we know it. *Journal of the Royal Society Interface*, **10 (86), 20130475**.

Friston, K. (2010). The free-energy principle: a unified brain theory? *Nature Reviews Neuroscience*, **11(2), 127–138**.

Friston, K., Mattout, J., & Kilner, J. (2011). Action understanding and active inference. *Biological Cybernetics*, **104(1–2), 137–160**.

Fritzman, J. M. & Thornburg, K. (2016). "I is someone else": Constituting the extended mind's fourth wave, with Hegel. *Essays in Philosophy*, **17(2), 156–190**.

Fuchs, T. & Röhricht, F. (2017). Schizophrenia and intersubjectivity: An embodied and enactive approach to psychopathology and psychotherapy. *Philosophy, Psychiatry, & Psychology*, **24(2), 127–142**.

Gallagher, S. (2005a). *How the Body Shapes the Mind*. Oxford: Oxford University Press.

Gallagher, S. (2005b). Metzinger's matrix: Living the virtual life with a real body. *Psyche*, **11(5), 1–9**.

Gallagher, S. (2013). The socially extended mind. *Cognitive Systems Research*, **25, 4–12**.

Gallagher, S. (2017). *Enactivist Interventions: Rethinking the Mind*. Oxford: Oxford University Press.

Gallagher, S. (2020). *Action and Interaction*. Oxford: Oxford University Press.

Gallagher, S. (2021). *Performance/Art: The Venetian Lectures*. Milan: Mimesis International Edizioni.

Gallagher, S. (2022). Surprise! Why enactivism and predictive processing are parting ways: The case of improvisation. *Possibility Studies and Society*. DOI: https://doi.org/10.1177/27538699221132691.

Gallagher, S. (2023). *The Self and Its Disorders*. Oxford: Oxford University Press.

Gallagher, S. & Allen, M. (2018). Active inference, enactivism and the hermeneutics of social cognition. *Synthese*, **195(6), 2627–2648**.

Gallagher, S. & Gallagher, J. (2020). Acting oneself as another: An actor's empathy for her character. *Topoi*, **39(4), 779–790**.

Gallagher, S. & Hutto, D. (2008). Understanding others through primary interaction and narrative practice. In J. Zlatev, T. Racine, C. Sinha, & E. Itkonen (eds.), *The Shared Mind: Perspectives on Intersubjectivity*. Amsterdam: John Benjamins, pp. **17–38**.

Gallagher, S., Hutto, D., Slaby, J. & Cole, J. (2013). The brain as part of an enactive system (commentary). *Behavioral and Brain Sciences*, **36(4), 421–422**.

Gallagher, S. & Lindgren, R. (2015). Enactive metaphors: Learning through full-body engagement. *Educational Psychology Review*, **27(3), 391–404**.

Gallagher, S., Mastrogiorgio, A. & Petracca, E. (2019). Economic reasoning and interaction in socially extended market institutions. *Frontiers in Psychology*, **10, 1856**. DOI: https://doi.org/10.3389/fpsyg.2019.01856.

Gallagher, S., Varga, S., & Sparaci, L. (2022). Disruptions of the meshed architecture in Autism Spectrum Disorder. *Psychoanalytic Inquiry*, **42(1), 76–95**.

Gallese, V. & Guerra, M. (2012). Embodying movies: Embodied simulation and film studies. *Cinema: Journal of Philosophy and the Moving Image*, **3, 183–210**.

Gangopadhyay, N. & Kiverstein, J. (2009). Enactivism and the unity of perception and action. *Topoi*, **28, 63–73**.

Garfield, J. L., Peterson, C.C., & Perry T. (2001). Social cognition, language acquisition and the development of the theory of mind. *Mind and Language*, **16, 494–541**.

Garfinkel, S., Minati, L., Gray, M. A. et al. (2014). Fear from the heart: Sensitivity to fear stimuli depends on individual heartbeats. *The Journal of Neuroscience*, **34(19), 6573–6582**.

Gibson, J. J. (1979). *The Ecological Approach to Visual Perception*. London: Psychology Press.

Glenberg, A. M. (2010). Embodiment as a unifying perspective for psychology. *Wiley Interdisciplinary Reviews: Cognitive Science*, **1(4), 586–596**.

Glenberg, A. M. & Kaschak, M. P. (2002). Grounding language in action. *Psychonomic Bulletin & Review*, **9, 558–565**.

Goldman, A. I. (2012). A moderate approach to embodied cognitive science. *Review of Philosophy and Psychology*, **3(1), 71–88**.

Goldman, A. I. (2014). The bodily formats approach to embodied cognition. In U. Kriegel (ed.), *Current Controversies in Philosophy of Mind*. New York and London: Routledge, pp. **91–108**.

Goldman, A. I. & Vignemont, de F. (2009). Is social cognition embodied? *Trends in Cognitive Sciences*, **13(4), 154–159**.

Goodwin, C. (2000). Action and embodiment within situated human interaction. *Journal of Pragmatics*, **32(10), 1489–1522**.

Gopnik, A. & Meltzoff, A. N. (1997). *Words, Thoughts and Theories*. Cambridge, MA: MIT Press.

Guajardo, N. R. & Watson, A. (2002). Narrative discourse and theory of mind development. *The Journal of Genetic Psychology*, **163, 305–325**.

Hafed, Z. M. & Krauzlis, R. J. (2006) Ongoing eye movements constrain visual perception. *Nature Neuroscience*, **9, 1449–1457**.

Halák, J. & Kříž, P. (2022). Phenomenological physiotherapy: Extending the concept of bodily intentionality. *Medical Humanities*, **48(4)**. DOI: https://doi .org/10.1136/medhum-2021-012300.

Halverson, C. A. (1995). Inside the cognitive workplace: New technology and air traffic control. (Doctoral dissertation, University of California, San Diego.)

Haugeland, J. (1991). Representational genera. In W. Ramsey, D. E. Rumelhart, & S. P. Stich, (eds.), *Philosophy and Connectionist Theory*. Hillsdale, NJ: Lawrence Erlbaum Associates, pp. **61–90**.

Haugeland, J. (1995). Mind embodied and embedded. In Y.-H. Houng & J.-C. Ho (eds.), *Mind and Cognition*. Taipei: Academia Sinica.

He, J. & Ravn, S. (2018). Sharing the dance: On the reciprocity of movement in the case of elite sports dancers. *Phenomenology and the Cognitive Sciences*, **17(1), 99–116**.

Heidegger, M. (1962). *Being and Time*, trans. J. Macquarrie & E. Robinson. New York: Harper and Row.

Helmholtz, H. (1962/1867). *Treatise on Physiological Optics*, 3rd ed., Vol. III, trans. J. Southall. New York: Dover.

Hobson, P. (2002). *The Cradle of Thought*. London: Macmillan.

Høffding, S. (2019). *A Phenomenology of Musical Absorption*. London: Palgrave Macmillan.

Hohwy, J. (2013). *The Predictive Mind*. Oxford: Oxford University Press.

Hohwy, J. (2016). The self-evidencing brain. *Nous*, **50(2), 259–285**.

Hohwy, J., Roepstorff, A., & Friston, K. (2008). Predictive coding explains binocular rivalry: An epistemological review. *Cognition*, **108(3), 687–701**.

Hurley, S. (1998). *Consciousness in Action*. Cambridge, MA: Harvard University Press.

Hurley, S. (2010). The varieties of externalism. In R. Menary (ed.), *The Extended Mind*. Cambridge, MA: MIT Press, pp. **101–153**.

Husserl, E. (1989). *Ideas Pertaining to a Pure Phenomenology and to a Phenomenological Philosophy – Second Book: Studies in the Phenomenology of Constitution*, trans. R. Rojcewicz & A. Schuwer. Dordrecht: Kluwer Academic.

Hutchins, E. (1995a). *Cognition in the Wild*. Cambridge, MA: MIT Press.

Hutchins, E. (1995b). How a cockpit remembers its speeds. *Cognitive Science*, **19(3), 265–288**.

Hutchins, E. (2000). Distributed cognition. In M. J. Smelzer & P. B. Baltes (eds.), *International Encyclopedia of the Social and Behavioral Sciences*. Amsterdam: Elsevier Science. https://arl.human.cornell.edu/linked%20docs/Hutchins_Distributed_Cognition.pdf .

Hutto, D. D. (2005) Knowing what? Radical versus conservative enactivism. *Phenomenology and the Cognitive Sciences*, **4(4), 389–405**.

Hutto, D. D. (2007). The narrative practice hypothesis. In D. D. Hutto (ed.), *Narrative and Understanding Persons*, Royal Institute of Philosophy Supplement. Cambridge: Cambridge University Press, pp. **43–68**.

Hutto, D. D. (2015). Overly enactive imagination? Radically re-imagining imagining. *The Southern Journal of Philosophy*, **53, 68–89**.

Hutto, D. D. & Abrahamson, D. (2022). Embodied, enactive education. In S. L. Macrine & J. Fugate (eds.), *Movement Matters: How Embodied Cognition Informs Teaching and Learning*. Cambridge, MA: MIT Press, pp. **39–54**.

Hutto, D. D. & Gallagher, S. (2017). Re-authoring narrative therapy: Improving our self-management tools. *Philosophy, Psychiatry, & Psychology*, **24(2), 157–167**.

Hutto, D. D., Kirchhoff, M. D., & Abrahamson, D. (2015). The enactive roots of STEM: Rethinking educational design in mathematics. *Educational Psychology Review*, **27(3), 371–389**.

Hutto, D. D., & Myin, E. (2013). *Radicalizing Enactivism: Basic Minds without Content*. Cambridge, MA: MIT Press.

Hutto, D. D. & Myin, E. (2020). Deflating deflationism about mental representation. In J. Smortchkova, K. Dołrega, & T. Schlicht (eds.), *What Are Mental Representations?* Oxford: Oxford University Press, pp. **79–100**.

Hutto, D. D. & Satne, G. (2015). The natural origins of content. *Philosophia*, **43** **(3), 521–536.**

Jackendoff, R. (2002). *Foundations of Language: Brain, Meaning, Grammar, Evolution.* Oxford: Oxford University Press.

Jäger, N., Schnädelbach, H., & Hale, J. (2016). Embodied interactions with adaptive architecture. In N. Dalton, H. Schnädelbach, M. Wiberg, & T. Varoudis (eds.), *Architecture and Interaction.* Cham: Springer, pp. **183–202.**

Jelić, A., Tieri, G., De Matteis, F., Babiloni, F., & Vecchiato, G. (2016). The enactive approach to architectural experience: A neurophysiological perspective on embodiment, motivation, and affordances. *Frontiers in Psychology*, **7, 481.**

Johnson, M. (1987). *The Body in the Mind: The Bodily Basis of Meaning, Imagination, and Reason.* Chicago: University of Chicago Press.

Johnson, M. (2015). The embodied meaning of architecture. In S. Robinson & J. Pallasmaa (eds.), *Mind in Architecture: Neuroscience, Embodiment, and the Future of Design.* Cambridge, MA: MIT Press, pp. **33–50.**

Johnson, M., & Lakoff, G. (2002). Why cognitive linguistics requires embodied realism. *Cognitive Linguistics*, **13(3), 245–263.**

Kelso, J. A. S. (2009). Coordination dynamics. In R. A. Meyers (ed.), *Encyclopedia of Complexity and Systems Science.* Heidelberg: Springer, pp. **1537–1564.** DOI: https://doi.org/10.1007/978-3-642-27737-5_101-3.

Kelso, J. A. S. (2014). Coordination dynamics and cognition. In K. Davids, R. Hristovski, D. Araújo D. et al. (eds.), *Routledge Research in Sport and Exercise Science. Complex Systems Sport.* London: Routledge/Taylor & Francis, pp. **18–43.**

Kilner, J. M., Friston, K. J., & Frith, C. D. (2007). Predictive coding: An account of the mirror neuron system. *Cognitive Processing*, **8(3), 159–166.**

Kirchhoff, M. D. (2012). Extended cognition and fixed properties: Steps to a third-wave version of extended cognition. *Phenomenology and the Cognitive Sciences*, **11, 287–308.**

Kirchhoff, M. D. (2017). From mutual manipulation to cognitive extension: Challenges and implications. *Phenomenology and the Cognitive Sciences*, **16 (5), 863–878.**

Kirchhoff, M. D. (2018). Autopoiesis, free energy, and the life–mind continuity thesis. *Synthese*, **195(6), 2519–2540.**

Kirchhoff, M. D. & Froese, T. (2017). Where there is life there is mind: In support of a strong life-mind continuity thesis. *Entropy*, **19(4), 169.**

Kirsh, D. & Maglio, P. (1994). On distinguishing epistemic from pragmatic action. *Cognitive Science*, **18(4), 513–549.**

Kiverstein, J. (2020). Free energy and the self: an ecological–enactive interpretation. *Topoi, 39*(**3**), **559–574**.

Kiverstein, J. & Rietveld, E. (2021). Scaling-up skilled intentionality to linguistic thought. *Synthese*, **198, 175–194**.

Knuuttila, T. & Voutilainen, A. (2003). A parser as an epistemic artifact: A material view on models. *Philosophy of Science*, **70(5), 1484–1495**.

Koch, S. C., Caldwell, C., & Fuchs, T. (2013). On body memory and embodied therapy. *Body, Movement and Dance in Psychotherapy*, **8(2), 82–94**.

Krickel, B. (2018). Saving the mutual manipulability account of constitutive relevance. *Studies in History and Philosophy of Science Part A*, **68, 58–67**.

Krueger, J. (2014). Affordances and the musically extended mind. *Frontiers in Psychology*, **4, 1003**.

Lakoff, G. & Johnson, M. (1999). *Philosophy in the Flesh: The Embodied Mind and Its Challenge to Western Thought*. New York: Basic Books.

Lakoff, G. & Núñez, R. (2000). *Where Mathematics Comes From*. New York: Basic Books.

Leong, V. & Schilbach, L. (2019). The promise of two-person neuroscience for developmental psychiatry: Using interaction-based sociometrics to identify disorders of social interaction. *British Journal of Psychiatry*, **215(5), 636–638**.

Lewes, G. H. (1879). The motor feelings and the muscular sense. In G. H. Lewes, *Problems of Life and Mind*. New York: Houghton, Mifflin and Company, pp. **312–328**.

Lindgren, R. & Bolling, A. (2013). Assessing the learning effects of interactive body metaphors in a mixed reality science simulation. In *Annual Meeting of the American Educational Research Association, San Francisco, CA*. Washington, DC: The American Educational Research Association, pp. **177–180**.

Lindgren, R. & Moshell, J. M. (2011). Supporting children's learning with body-based metaphors in a mixed reality environment. In *Proceedings of the 10th International Conference on Interaction Design and Children*, Ann Arbor, MI: ACM, pp. **177–180**.

Malafouris, L. (2013). *How Things Shape the Mind*. Cambridge, MA: MIT Press.

Maturana, H. & Varela, F. (1980/1972). *Autopoiesis and Cognition: The Realization of the Living*. Dordrecht: D. Reidel.

Meltzoff, A. N., Ramírez, R. R., Saby, J. N. et al. (2018). Infant brain responses to felt and observed touch of hands and feet: An MEG study. *Developmental Science*, **21(5), e12651**.

Menary, R. (2007). *Cognitive Integration: Mind and Cognition Unbounded.* Basingstoke: Palgrave Macmillan.

Menary, R. (ed.) (2010a). *The Extended Mind.* Cambridge, MA: MIT Press.

Menary, R. (2010b). Cognitive integration and the extended mind. In R. Menary (ed.), *The Extended Mind.* Cambridge, MA: MIT Press, pp. **227–243**.

Menary, R. (2010c). Introduction to the special issue on 4E cognition. *Phenomenology and the Cognitive Sciences*, **9(4), 459–463**.

Merleau-Ponty, M. (2012). *Phenomenology of Perception*, trans. D. Landes. London: Routledge.

Merritt, M. (2015). Thinking-is-moving: Dance, agency, and a radically enactive mind. *Phenomenology and the Cognitive Sciences*, **14(1), 95–110**.

Millikan, R. (1991). Perceptual content and Fregean myth. *Mind*, **100(4), 439–459**.

Millikan, R. G. (1995). Pushmi-pullyu representations. *Philosophical Perspectives*, **9, 185–200**.

Miyazono, K. (2017). Does functionalism entail extended mind? *Synthese*, **194 (9), 3523–3541**.

Murray, L. & Trevarthen, C. (1985). Emotional regulation of interactions between 2-month-olds and their mothers. In T. M. Field & N. A. Fox (eds.), *Social Perception in Infants.* Norwood, NJ: Ablex, pp. **177–197**.

Natvik, E., Groven, K. S., Råheim, M., Gjengedal, E., & Gallagher, S. (2019). Space perception, movement, and insight: Attuning to the space of everyday life after major weight loss. *Physiotherapy Theory and Practice*, **35(2), 101–108**.

Nelson, K. (2003). Narrative and the emergence of a consciousness of self. In G. D. Fireman, T. E. J. McVay, & O. Flanagan (eds.), *Narrative and Consciousness.* Oxford: Oxford University Press, pp. **17–36**.

Nelson, K. (2007). *Young Minds in Social Worlds.* Cambridge, MA: Harvard University Press.

Newen, A. , De Bruin, L. , & Gallagher, S. (eds.). (2018). *Oxford Handbook of 4E-Cognition.* Oxford: Oxford University Press.

Noë, A. (2004). *Action in Perception.* Cambridge, MA: MIT Press.

Øberg, G. K., Normann, B., & Gallagher, S. (2015). Embodied-enactive clinical reasoning in physical therapy. *Physiotherapy Theory and Practice*, **31(4), 244–252**.

Onishi, K. H. & Baillargeon, R. (2005). Do 15-month-old infants understand false beliefs? *Science*, **308(5719), 255–258**.

O'Regan, J. K. & Noë, A. (2001). A sensorimotor account of vision and visual consciousness. *Behavioral and Brain Sciences*, **24(5), 939–973**.

Oullier, O. & Basso, F. (2010). Embodied economics: How bodily information shapes the social coordination dynamics of decision-making. *Philosophical Transactions of the Royal Society B: Biological Sciences*, **365(1538)**, 291–301.

Palermos, S. O. (2014). Loops, constitution, and cognitive extension. *Cognitive Systems Research*, **27, 25–41**.

Parr, T., Da Costa, L., & Friston, K. (2020). Markov blankets, information geometry and stochastic thermodynamics. *Philosophical Transactions of the Royal Society A*, **378(2164), 20190159**.

Peirce, C. S. (1887). Logical machines. *American Journal of Psychology*, **1(1), 165–170**.

Peirce, C. S. (1931–1935, 1958). *Collected Papers of C. S. Peirce*, eds. C. Hartshorne, P. Weiss, & A. Burks. Cambridge, MA: Harvard University Press (abbreviated: CP followed by the conventional "[volume].[page]" notation).

Peirce, C. S. (1958). *Collected Papers of C.S. Peirce. Vol 7*. Ed. A. W. Burks. Cambridge, MA: Harvard University Press.

Perner, J. (1992). Grasping the concept of representation: Its impact on 4-year-olds' theory of mind and beyond. *Human Development*, **35(3), 146–155**.

Perry, M. (2003). Distributed cognition. In J. Carroll (ed.), *HCI Models, Theories, and Frameworks: Toward a Multidisciplinary Science*. Amsterdam: Elsevier, pp. **193–223**.

Petracca, E. (2021). Embodying bounded rationality: From embodied bounded rationality to embodied rationality. *Frontiers in Psychology*, **12, 710607**.

Petracca, E. & Gallagher, S. (2020). Economic cognitive institutions. *Journal of Institutional Economics*, **16(6), 747–765**.

Prinz, J. (2009). Is consciousness embodied? In P. Robbins & M. Aydede (eds.), *Cambridge Handbook of Situated Cognition*. Cambridge: Cambridge University Press, pp. **419–437**.

Prinz, J. (2006). Putting the brakes on enactive perception. *Psyche*, **12, 1–19**.

Proffitt, D. R. (2006). Embodied perception and the economy of action. *Perspectives on Psychological Science*, **1(2), 110–122**.

Proffitt, D. R., Bhalla, M., Gossweiler, R., & Midgett, J. (1995). Perceiving geographical slant. *Psychonomic Bulletin & Review*, **2, 409–428**.

Pulvermüller, F. (2005). Brain mechanisms linking language and action. *Nature Reviews Neuroscience*, **6(7), 576–582**.

Ramsey, W. (2007). *Representation Reconsidered*. Cambridge: Cambridge University Press.

Ramsey, W. (2020). Defending representation realism. In J. Smortchkova, K. Dołrega, & T. Schlicht (eds.), *What Are Mental Representations?* Oxford: Oxford University Press, pp. **54–78**.

Ramstead, M. J., Kirchhoff, M. D., Constant, A., & Friston, K. J. (2021). Multiscale integration: Beyond internalism and externalism. *Synthese*, **198** **(1), 41–70**.

Ravn, S. (2016). Embodying interaction in Argentinean tango and sports dance. In T. DeFrantz & P. Rothfield (eds.), *Choreography and Corporeality: Relay in Motion*. London: Palgrave Macmillan pp. **119–134**.

Ravn, S. & Høffding, S. (2021). Improvisation and thinking in movement: An enactivist analysis of agency in artistic practices. *Phenomenology and the Cognitive Sciences* **21, 515–537**. DOI: https://doi.org/10.1007/s11097-021-09756-9.

Rietveld, E. & Brouwers, A. A. (2017). Optimal grip on affordances in architectural design practices: An ethnography. *Phenomenology and the Cognitive Sciences*, **16(3), 545–564**.

Rietveld, E. & Kiverstein, J. (2014). A rich landscape of affordances. *Ecological Psychology*, **26(4), 325–352**.

Robbins, P. & Aydede, M. (2009). A short primer on situated cognition. In P. Robbins & M. Aydede (eds.), *The Cambridge Handbook of Situated Cognition*. Cambridge, Cambridge University Press, pp. **1–16**.

Rock, I. & Harris, C. S. (1967). Vision and touch. *Scientific American*, **216(5), 96–104**.

Röhricht, F., Gallagher, S., Geuter, U., & Hutto, D. D. (2014). Embodied cognition and body psychotherapy: The construction of new therapeutic environments. *Sensoria: A Journal of Mind, Brain & Culture*, **10(1), n.p**.

Roll, J-P. & Roll, R. (1988). From eye to foot: A proprioceptive chain involved in postural control. In G. Amblard, A. Berthoz, & F. Clarac (eds.), *Posture and Gait: Development, Adaptation, and Modulation*. Amsterdam: Excerpta Medica, pp. **155–164**.

Rolla, G. & Novaes, F. (2022). Ecological-enactive scientific cognition: Modeling and material engagement. *Phenomenology and the Cognitive Sciences*, **21(3), 625–643** DOI: https://doi.org/10.1007/s11097-020-09713-y.

Rowlands, M. (2006) *Body Language*. Cambridge, MA: MIT Press.

Rowlands, M. (2009). The extended mind. *Zygon*, **44(3), 628–641**.

Rowlands, M. (2010). *The New Science of the Mind: From Extended Mind to Embodied Phenomenology*. Cambridge, MA: MIT Press.

Rubio-Fernández, P. & Geurts, B. (2013). How to pass the false-belief task before your fourth birthday. *Psychological Science*, **24(1), 27–33**.

Rupert, R. (2004). Challenges to the hypothesis of extended cognition. *Journal of Philosophy* **101, 389–428**.

Rupert, R. (2011). Embodiment, consciousness, and the massively representational mind. *Philosophical Topics*, **39(1), 99–120**.

Ryan, K. & Gallagher, S. (2020). Between ecological psychology and enactivism: Is there resonance? *Frontiers in Psychology*, **11**, **1147**. DOI: https://doi.org/10.3389/fpsyg.2020.01147.

Saxe, R. & Kanwisher, N. (2003). People thinking about thinking people: The role of the temporo-parietal junction in "theory of mind." *Neuroimage*, **19(4)**, **1835–1842**.

Schiavio, A. & Høffding, S. (2015). Playing together without communicating? A pre-reflective and enactive account of joint musical performance. *Musicae Scientiae*, **19(4)**, **366–388**.

Schwartenbeck, P., FitzGerald, T., Dolan, R. J., & Friston, K. (2013) Exploration, novelty, surprise, and free energy minimization. *Frontiers in Psychology*, **4**, **710**. DOI: https://doi.org/10.3389/fpsyg.2013.00710.

Shapiro, L. (2004). *The Mind Incarnate*. Cambridge, MA: MIT Press.

Shapiro, L. (2007). The embodied cognition research programme. *Philosophy Compass*, **2(2)**, **338–346**.

Shapiro, L. (2014). Book review: *Radicalizing Enactivism: Basic Minds without Content*. *Mind*, **123(489)**, **213–220**.

Shapiro, L. & Spaulding, S. (2021). Embodied cognition. *The Stanford Encyclopedia of Philosophy*, ed. E. Zalta. https://plato.stanford.edu/archives/win2021/entries/embodied-cognition/.

Shea, N. (2018). *Representation in Cognitive Science*. Oxford: Oxford University Press.

Skulmowski, A. & Rey, G. D. (2018). Embodied learning: Introducing a taxonomy based on bodily engagement and task integration. *Cognitive Research: Principles and Implications*, **3(1)**, **1–10**.

Smith, B. C. (1996). *On the Origin of Objects*. Cambridge, MA: MIT Press.

Smortchkova, J., Dołrega, K., & Schlicht, T. (eds.) (2020). *What Are Mental Representations?* Oxford: Oxford University Press.

Soto-Andrade, J. (2018). Enactive metaphorising in the learning of mathematics. In G. Kaiser, H. Forgasz, M. Graven et al. (eds.), *Invited Lectures from the 13th International Congress on Mathematical Education*. Cham: Springer, pp. **619–637**.

Sprevak, M. (2009). Extended cognition and functionalism. *Journal of Philosophy*, **106(9)**, **503–527**.

Stapleton, M. (2013). Steps to a "properly embodied" cognitive science. *Cognitive Systems Research*, **22–23**, **1–11**.

Sterelny, K. (2010). Minds: Extended or scaffolded? *Phenomenology and the Cognitive Sciences*, **9(4)**, **465–481**.

Sutton, J. (2010). Exograms and interdisciplinarity: History, the extended mind and the civilizing process. In R. Menary (ed.), *The Extended Mind*. Cambridge, MA: MIT Press, pp. **189–225**.

Sutton, J. & Tribble, E. (2011). Cognitive ecology as a framework for Shakespearean studies. *Shakespeare Studies*, **39, 94–103**.

Thompson, E. (2005). Sensorimotor subjectivity and the enactive approach to experience. *Phenomenology and the Cognitive Sciences*, **4(4), 407–427**.

Thompson, E. (2007). *Mind in Life: Biology, Phenomenology and the Sciences of Mind*, Cambridge, MA: Harvard University Press.

Thompson, E. & Varela, F. (2001). Radical embodiment: Neural dynamics and consciousness. *Trends in Cognitive Sciences* **5(10), 418–425**.

Tognoli, E. & Kelso, J. A. S (2015). The coordination dynamics of social neuromarkers. *Frontiers in Human Neuroscience*, **9, 563**. DOI: https://doi .org/10.3389/fnhum.2015.00563.

Tognoli, E., Zhang, M., Fuchs, A., Beetle, C., & Kelso, J. A. S. (2020). Coordination dynamics: A foundation for understanding social behavior. *Frontiers in Human Neuroscience*, **14, 317**. DOI: https://doi.org/10.3389 /fnhum.2020.00317.

Trevarthen, C. (1979). Communication and cooperation in early infancy: A description of primary intersubjectivity. In M. Bullowa (ed.), *Before Speech*. Cambridge: Cambridge University Press, pp. **321–348**.

Trevarthen, C. & Hubley, P. (1978). Secondary intersubjectivity: Confidence, confiding and acts of meaning in the first year. In A. Lock (ed.), *Action, Gesture and Symbol: The Emergence of Language*. London: Academic Press, pp. **183–229**.

Tribble, E. (2011). *Cognition in the Globe: Attention and Memory in Shakespeare's Theatre*. Berlin: Springer.

Tsakiris, M. (2010). My body in the brain: A neurocognitive model of body-ownership. *Neuropsychologia*, **48(3), 703–712**.

Van Den Herik, J. C. (2018). Attentional actions: An ecological-enactive account of utterances of concrete words. *Psychology of Language and Communication*, **22(1), 90–123**.

Van Der Schyff, D., Schiavio, A., Walton, A., Velardo, V., & Chemero, A. (2018). Musical creativity and the embodied mind: Exploring the possibilities of 4E cognition and dynamical systems theory. *Music & Science*, **1, 1–18**, https://doi.org/10.1177/2059204318792319.

Varela, F. J. (1996). Neurophenomenology: A methodological remedy for the hard problem. *Journal of Consciousness Studies*, **3(4), 330–349**.

Varela, F. J. (1999) Present-time consciousness. *Journal of Consciousness Studies*, **6(2–3), 111–140**.

Varela, F. J., Thompson, E., & Rosch, E. (1991). *The Embodied Mind: Cognitive Science and Human Experience*. Cambridge: MIT Press.

Varga, S. (2018). Interpersonal judgments, embodied reasoning, and juridical legitimacy. In A. Newen, L. de Bruin, & S. Gallagher (eds.), *The Oxford Handbook of 4E Cognition*. Oxford: Oxford University Press, pp. **863–874**.

Varga, S. & Heck, D. H. (2017). Rhythms of the body, rhythms of the brain: Respiration, neural oscillations, and embodied cognition. *Consciousness and Cognition*, **56, 77–90**.

Wadham, J. (2016). Common-sense functionalism and the extended mind. *Philosophical Quarterly*, **66 (262), 136–151**.

Ward, D., Silverman, D., & Villalobos, M. (2017). Introduction: The varieties of enactivism. *Topoi*, **36(3), 365–375**.

Wheeler, M. (2005). *Reconstructing the Cognitive World*. Cambridge, MA: MIT Press.

Wheeler, M. (2012). Minds, things and materiality. In J. Schulkin (ed.), *Action, Perception and the Brain*. Basingstoke: Palgrave-Macmillan, pp. **147–163**.

Wheeler, M. (2018). Talking about more than heads: The embodied, embedded and extended creative mind. In B. Gaut & M. Kieran (eds.), *Creativity and Philosophy*. London: Routledge, pp. **230–250**.

Wheeler, M. (2019). Breaking the waves: Beyond parity and complementarity in the arguments for extended cognition. In M. Colombo, L. Irvine, & M. Stapleton (eds.), *Andy Clark and Critics*. Oxford: Oxford University Press, pp. **81–97**.

Wheeler, M. & Clark, A. (2008) Culture, embodiment and genes: Unravelling the triple helix. *Philosophical Transactions of the Royal Society Series B*, **363, 3563–3575**.

Wiese, W. & Friston, K. (2021). Examining the continuity between life and mind: Is there a continuity between autopoietic intentionality and representationality? *Philosophies*, **6(1), 1–18**.

Wilson, M. (2002). Six views of embodied cognition. *Psychonomic Bulletin & Review*, **9(4), 625–636**.

Wimmer, H. & Perner, J. (1983). Beliefs about beliefs: Representation and constraining function of wrong beliefs in young children's understanding of deception. *Cognition*, **13(1), 103–128**.

Woodward, J. (2003). *Making Things Happen: A Theory of Causal Explanation*. Oxford: Oxford University Press.

Yarbus, A. (1967). *Eye Movements and Vision*. New York: Plenum Press.

Zahidi, K. & Myin, E. (2016). Radically enactive numerical cognition. In G. Etzelmuller & C. Tewes (eds.), *Embodiment in Evolution and Culture*. Tübingen: Mohr Siebeck, pp. **57–71**.

Zelano, C., Jiang, H., Zhou, G. et al. (2016). Nasal respiration entrains human limbic oscillations and modulates cognitive function. *Journal of Neuroscience*, **36(49), 12448–12467**.

Zhang, M., Kalies, W. D., Kelso, J. S., & Tognoli, E. (2020). Topological portraits of multiscale coordination dynamics. *Journal of Neuroscience Methods*, **339, 108672**.

Ziemke, T. (2001). Are robots embodied. *Modeling Cognitive Development in Robotic Systems*, **85, 701–746**.

Zlatev, J. (2010). Phenomenology and cognitive linguistics. In S. Gallagher & D. Schmicking (eds.), *Handbook of Phenomenology and Cognitive Science*. Dordrecht: Springer, **415–443**.

Philosophy of Mind

Keith Frankish
The University of Sheffield

Keith Frankish is a philosopher specializing in philosophy of mind, philosophy of psychology, and philosophy of cognitive science. He is the author of *Mind and Supermind* (Cambridge University Press, 2004) and *Consciousness* (2005), and has also edited or coedited several collections of essays, including *The Cambridge Handbook of Cognitive Science* (Cambridge University Press, 2012), *The Cambridge Handbook of Artificial Intelligence* (Cambridge University Press, 2014) (both with William Ramsey), and *Illusionism as a Theory of Consciousness* (2017).

About the Series

This series provides concise, authoritative introductions to contemporary work in philosophy of mind, written by leading researchers and including both established and emerging topics. It provides an entry point to the primary literature and will be the standard resource for researchers, students, and anyone wanting a firm grounding in this fascinating field.

Cambridge Elements ☰

Philosophy of Mind

Elements in the Series

A full series listing is available at: www.cambridge.org/EPMI

Printed in the United States
by Baker & Taylor Publisher Services